MARKET YOURSELF

MARKET YOURSELF

A MARKETING SYSTEM FOR SMART AND CREATIVE BUSINESS OWNERS

TARA SWIGER

COOPERATIVE PRESS
Cleveland, Ohio

Library of Congress Control Number: 2012938687
ISBN 13: 978-1-937513-08-5
First Edition

Published by Cooperative Press
http://www.cooperativepress.com

Every effort has been made to ensure that all the information in this book is accurate at the time of publication, however Cooperative Press neither endorses nor guarantees the content of external links referenced in this book.

If you have questions or comments about this book, or need information about licensing, custom editions, special sales, or academic/corporate purchases, please contact Cooperative Press: info@cooperativepress.com or 13000 Athens Ave C288, Lakewood, OH 44107 USA

FOR COOPERATIVE PRESS

Senior Editor: Shannon Okey
Development Editor: Heather Ordover
Assistant Editor: Elizabeth Green Musselman

TO JAY

TABLE OF CONTENTS

INTRODUCTION

You make something by hand. It is glorious and lovely and altogether wonderful.

What it lacks is *people*. People who are buying it, begging for it, and talking about it.

If this is you, if you make something delightful but don't have the people (or enough of them), then this book is for you.

You, the lover of handmade. You, the maker. You, the business owner.

If you are fabulous at making your thing, but don't have (enough) people, then this book will teach you how to speak to them, attract them, and keep them coming back.

If you've been selling for any amount of time, you've learned that simply making your thing and putting it online (or bringing it to a show) isn't enough. Without a clear label, no one will buy it. Without a compelling description, no one will buy it. Without you sharing it, no one will find it. Without being reminded, even the biggest fan won't return.

All of this is marketing.

It's sharing your thing with the people who will love it.

In this book, we're going to take the noun *marketing* (which has a bad reputation for being slimy), and turn it into a verb, *marketing*, something do-able in a non-gross way.

MY MARKETING JOURNEY

Five years ago my knitting obsession turned into a dyeing and spinning obsession. Marketing what I made helped turn my hobby into a business, and three years later I quit my day job because my business made enough to support my family. It was a slow path that started simply. Looking back, three years seems like nothing… but when you're bouncing around in horrible office temp jobs, it feels like an eternity.

It all started one bright February day, I walked into a yarn shop with one of my hand-dyed skeins in hand, looking for a matching skein. The yarn shop owner gushed, "Could you dye some custom skeins for my shop?!"

Of course!
(I had no idea if I could or not!)

I walked back to my car with an armload of undyed yarn, supplied by the yarn shop owner. I came back two weeks later with her dyed skeins (wrapped in my quickly home-printed label) and a few more samples of what I could make for her.

And Blonde Chicken Boutique, my goofily-named business, was born.

I continued to dye for that shop even after I moved away that summer. I thought I'd look for a few local shops and expand. But before I could, my mom wore my hand-dyed, hand-spun, hand-knit shawl into an art supply store and (of course!) bragged how her daughter had made it. (Mom: my first advertiser.) In October, the owner asked me to bring in some yarn. I brought in 20 skeins to sell on consignment. (She'd pay me when they sold.)

They never really sold (a few maybe?), but that gave me the confidence I needed. I took the unsold skeins and listed them on Etsy that November. And again, none sold. I realized that no one knew I had yarns for sale, and I needed some way of telling people. Of meeting people and *then* telling them. I started a blog (or rather, turned my personal knitting blog into one that talked a bit more about what I was selling). In December, I got a custom order for $90 worth of yarn (a fortune!).

In January (nearly one year after my business "started"), I launched my first planned marketing effort: The Month of Love. I publicly committed to spinning a yarn every day from January 14th to February 14th, each yarn inspired by a famous couple. Best of all, I solicited couple/color ideas. I would spin YOUR suggestions and then give you 50% off any skein you wanted, to thank you for helping me design a yarn.

That was it.

People were delighted and linked to it. They commented. I gave discounts and people purchased. For the first time, I had people. I could imagine who was buying, and I started talked directly to them (on the blog, in emails, in descriptions).

I listened to them.
I used the language they used.
I replied and commented and made every effort to get to know *every* customer I could.

HOW TO USE THIS BOOK

This is not a rule book; it's a handbook, a playbook, a *work*book.

Reading any part of it (no matter how brilliant) won't change your business—only you will!

To get the most out of this book, grab a pen and a notebook every time you pick it up. You'll find worksheets sprinkled throughout the book. A full 98% percent of the book's value rests in *you* doing the worksheets.

After that first Month of Love, as long as I made yarn (and made it available), I sold yarn. The more I worked *with* my customers, the more I sold.

> *Even when I adjusted my pricing to reflect what I needed to make a profit.*
> *Even when I branched into selling fiber for spinners.*

As long as I kept talking to my customers, I sold yarn online, in yarn shops, and at craft shows.

After a year of selling whatever I could make, I set some goals for what I'd need to have in order to quit my day job, and I did it. I celebrated my quitting publicly and that brought more questions from crafters than from yarn lovers.

When I was spending more time talking to crafty businesses than I was to yarn lovers, I decided to answer all the questions at once and held my first class: Share Your Thing. That class led to more classes, a whole separate site for crafty businesses (TaraSwiger.com), and working one-on-one with crafters to shape their next steps.

All the while, I have kept using Blonde Chicken Boutique as my own laboratory. It has grown and changed and shifted, and it still teaches me something new every month. Thanks to the same sweet customers, Blonde Chicken Boutique yarn is available once a month online and (all the time) in local yarn shops around the world. (Yes, even in New Zealand!)

Now I experiment with other craft businesses as much as my own… and that led me here, to compile everything I've learned by experimenting, measuring, and working hard, both in my own business and in others like yours.

I know why you're here.
You're asking: What should I do to get more buyers?

The answer isn't ONE thing: it's a system of actions; it's a strategy; it's a day-by-day plan. Even better (or more frustrating for people who want a quick answer), it depends entirely on who you are, what your product is, and who your people are. There is no one-size-fits-all system, but there is a process you can use to find your *own* system—the one that works for you—and your people and the life you want.

It's my hope that this book lays out that process and helps you create your own system.
It's my hope that this book meets you where you are and helps you lay out the map to get you where you want to be.
It's my hope that, when it does, you'll let me know.

Happy adventures,

Tara

EMAIL ME ANYTIME:
TARA@TARASWIGER.COM

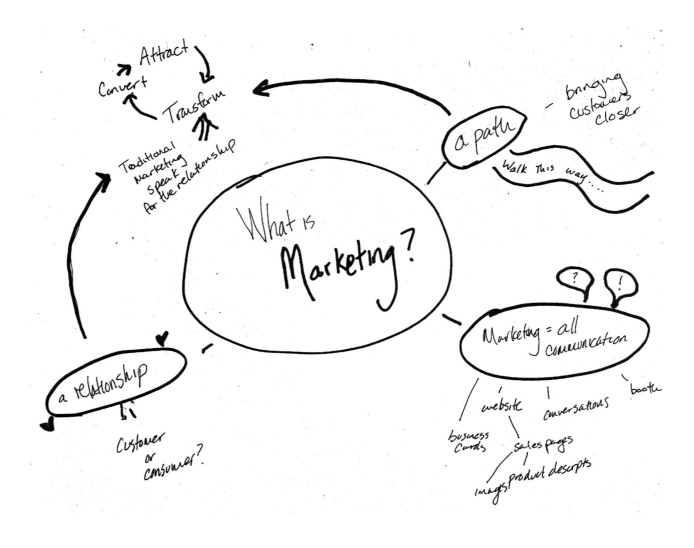

Attract
Convert
Transform

Traditional Marketing speak for the relationship

a path

— bringing customers closer

Walk This way....

What is Marketing?

a relationship

Customer or consumer?

Marketing = all communication

? !

website
business cards
conversations
sales pages
booth
images
product descripts

CHAPTER 1: WHAT IS MARKETING?

MARKETING IS ANY COMMUNICATION YOU HAVE WITH YOUR PEOPLE*

It's your **email signature**.
It's your **product description**.
It's your **blog**, your **Twitter stream**, your **Facebook page**.
It's your **booth** at a craft show.
It's even your *outfit* at a craft show.

Marketing is more than an opportunity to tell your people about your product. It's an opportunity to tell them what makes it (and you) different.

Marketing is, simply, communicating to people who want to buy your thing.

The people who want your thing are your Right People and here's the great news: you only have to talk to these people. *(Really!)*

> You do not have to aim your marketing ray gun (pew! pew!) at anyone else.
> You do not have to sell ice to Eskimos.
> You do not have to sell to people who don't want what you make—or who don't know they want it.

I know, I *know*, when you want to share your thing with the Whole Wild World, it seems insane to just dismiss a whole segment of the population. But you are just you, you're not a multinational corporation (and if you are, why are you reading this book?) so you don't have the money and manpower to convert people who aren't open to your product.

But here's the secret sauce: focusing your marketing effort on just your Right People will save you time, money, and sanity. It will make your working life a delight (everyone you interact with loves you!) and will save you money in returns, ad buys and angst. (Angst takes up too much productive time.)

We'll talk more about Right People in Chapter 3, but I want you to keep the concept in mind as we discuss what marketing *can* be. In every instance of what marketing is (and how it can work), we always mean *for your Right People*.

---

* *Your people:* the people who want what you're selling. We'll get into more of this in the next chapter.

MARKETING AS A PATH

I just told you that marketing = *any* communication. To keep that communication clear and to make sure your Right Person is both receiving and understanding the message, you'll want to create a marketing *strategy*.

Think of this strategy as a path that you're laying before your Right Person. You want her to find her way from wherever she is (in relation to your business) to becoming a loyal and delighted customer. To help her get there, you'll lay out a clear, easy-to-navigate path.

Your business is unique and will have its own particular path, but it will include some basic elements. For example, no matter what your business is or who your Right Person is, you'll want her to move deeper into her relationship with you (from not knowing about you to being a raving fan). In this relationship, there are several recognizable levels.

Let's look at some of the ways you can think about this path that your Right People will take.

MARKETING AS A RELATIONSHIP

In communicating with your Right People, you'll be building relationships with them. As the relationship deepens, your Right Person will move through the following steps:

1. A potential customer has a problem or is looking for something and comes in contact with your business.
2. A potential customer becomes a consumer as she continues to get to know you (reading your blog, getting emails, postcards, etc.).
3. A customer buys and continues a relationship with you.

The traditional "marketing" way of stating this relationship is…

Attract: Bring people to your thing.
Convert: Convince them to buy.
Transform: Turn customers into telling-their-friends fans.

Every bit of your communication, every smackeral of your marketing should move your Right Person from one step the next. Everything you work on, everything you say should serve to build a relationship with the Right Person, so they move closer to either becoming a customer or becoming a repeat customer (and evangelist).

You'll use these relationship steps in Chapter 7 when we create a strategy for your marketing. Until then, keep them in mind as you read this book and think about your marketing. You can use the path metaphor as a tool for measuring any marketing decisions you make, and you can use it to decide what tools will work best for your business.

One more thing to consider before we get into the specific marketing tools you'll use: there's a difference between a customer and a consumer (especially in the online world). A **consumer** reads your blog and interacts with you or your business in some way, but a **customer** *buys*.

A Twitter follower is a consumer. An email subscriber is a consumer. A *customer* forks over their money for your delightful product. The job of your marketing is to turn strangers into consumers and consumers into customers. The offline example of a consumer would be someone who comes into your shop regularly and comments on how much they love everything, but never buys.

Some consumers will never become customers. These people are not your Right People. (It doesn't mean they're *wrong*, they just aren't going to support you and thus, they're not who you want to spend time seducing.) Consumers can be encouraging (especially when you first get started), but simply growing your consumer base won't create a sustainable business. You have to have some way of turning those consumers into customers.

One of the risks of an online business is that it's very easy to focus on getting more consumers: blog subscribers, Twitter followers, and Facebook fans. Those numbers are easy to see (and they can be public, social proof of your awesomeness). But marketing that only brings you more consumers will bankrupt you. **You'll be popular, but broke.**

The aim of all the marketing that you do from this day forward will be based on the idea that you're going to turn strangers into consumers, and transform consumers into customers. When you find yourself looking for more consumers (Twitter followers, blog readers, and commenters), stop and reassess: "Are these consumers becoming customers? If not, how can I move them down that path?" (We'll talk more about this in Chapter 4 and 7, but keep it in mind for now.)

YOU, NOT THEM

Throughout the book, we're going to start nearly every adventure by looking at you and your product. We're going to dig deep into what makes you and your product different, long before we talk about your people, your "target market."

Why?

As a maker-of-things, your hands, your vision, and your *you-ness* is at the heart of what you're selling.

Until you get ultra-clear on what you are bringing to your craft, you won't be able to communicate that to buyers. Until you know what is unique about the way you do it, you won't have a clear and compelling message.

If you start this process thinking about Other People, you will diffuse the you-ness. The message will get muddy and unclear. Your message will be boring and corporate. The world doesn't need more of what's out there already; it needs your take on your craft, *your* particular vision of the world.

Bonus!
The more YOU you infuse into your work, the easier it will be for the Right People to find you. The people who get the way you work and who love the way you express yourself will flock to your thing. Everyone else (all those people who wouldn't like what you make) will be filtered out. If you're worried about more customers, this might seem counter-intuitive (you want to sell to *everyone*), but trust me, you do *not want to sell to everyone*. You do not want to sell to people who will return it. You do not want to attract readers who will be turned off when they discover the real you. You want your business to be filled with people who get it and want to buy it.

THEM, NOT YOU
Once you're clear on what you bring and what *your* vision is, we'll flip to talking about *your* people. We'll look at how to find out what they want (and how to find them), then how you give them what you want.

The sweet spot is where what you do matches up with what other people want.

To get you to that sweet spot, we've got to measure equal parts *your awesomeness* with equal parts *Your People*.

Most crafters I work with find it easy to focus on one aspect, and tricky to switch to thinking about the other. It can be a challenge, and will occasionally feel like a conflict. To help you through this, we're going to focus entirely on *you* in Chapter 2, and then entirely on *your people* in Chapter 3. In all the other chapters, I'll remind you to flip back and forth between the two.

The thing to remember now is that there is no conflict. It's a process, not a one-time answer. As you focus on what you're great at doing, learn the way to communicate it, and listen deeply to your people, you'll find your way to that sweet spot.

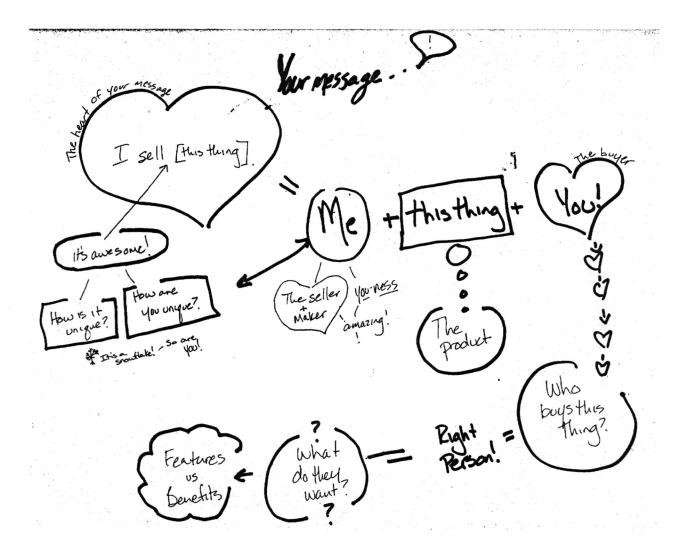

CHAPTER 2: GETTING STARTED — YOUR MESSAGE

Now that you know that marketing is *all* of your communication and you understand that it's a path you're building for your Right Person, the obvious question is: where to start?

We'll start at the core:
1. Your message (what it IS)
2. Your People (who wants it)
3. How you deliver your message (tone, pictures, etc.)
4. Your home (where your message lives)

Once you have these core pieces in place, you can venture through the world, knowing that your message and your brand represent what you want them to represent. We'll cover your message in this chapter, move on to your Right People in the next, then get into communicating your message in Chapter 4.

If you're just starting your business, you can walk through these areas step-by-step, work out everywhere that your message will show up and plan it right from the start, but know that flexibility is key. There'll be surprises you never imagined! If you're already in business *in any way*, you have already created many of these pieces (whether you know it not). Part of your challenge in getting to the core will be deciding what you *want* that core to be and to recognize what it already is. Sometimes you'll be surprised at how different the two are, but (hopefully) most of the time you'll be delighted at how clearly your message is already being communicated.

No matter where your business is, this chapter is the heart of all your marketing and I strongly encourage you to work through it before you read anything else.

YOUR MESSAGE

Your message is, very simply, *I sell this thing*.

If you aren't clearly saying *I sell X* (and fill in X with a clear description of what you sell) on your website, your business cards, and anything that represents your company… then no amount of marketing is going to result in sales. At a very basic level, *I sell X* should be clear to everyone who comes in contact with your marketing.

But simply saying *I sell this thing* is much too boring. It's not going to help your thing stand out from anyone else's thing. We're going to get to the heart of what your thing is (and why the person hearing the message even cares), while not clouding or obscuring the basic statement.

Let's expand that earlier statement. Your message really is: **I sell this awesome thing** (and here's why you care). You have to replace "awesome" with a clear description of what makes your thing completely different from everything else. To do that, **you are going to have to be clear on what is different and wonderful about your thing.**

And the answer is not, "Because I hand-made it."

The answer is in the question: what is unique to *you*?
- What about your thing is so completely *you* that no one else could ever do it?
- What about *how* you made it is different?
- What makes it unusual or interesting?

What you will need to answer those questions:
- qualities of your product (eco-friendly, colorful, child-friendly, etc.)
- qualities of YOU (are you bubbly, shy, misanthropic?)
- visual style (colors, photography, illustration)
- verbal style (tone, word choice)

In the message above, you'll see that it's made up of three parts:
1. I
2. this thing
3. why you care

Once you identify your style, you can see how it influences what you make. You can communicate its specialness. Together, these qualities will start to inform your brand (the personality of your company), and will be applied everywhere else in your business.

YOU
You are a delightful, unique snowflake (*it's true!*) and you are at the heart of what makes your business exist. Only by infusing every aspect of your business with *you* will you be able to reach and communicate with the people who love it. From your tone of voice to the colors you use, a successful brand is cohesive. And the easiest way to be cohesive is to be *you*, to pick colors you like, speak in a voice that comes naturally, and style your work in a way that appeals to *you*.

You might already have a good idea of your particular style and voice. *Wonderful.* However, you still need to write it down, to clarify it, so you always have it handy.

The qualities you specify in the following worksheet will help you craft your core message, and will in turn affect every aspect of your communication. You will keep the tone in mind when you write descriptions; you'll shoot photographs with your visual style; and you'll create ads that reflect the qualities of you and your brand.

So, in other words, don't skip this!

WORKSHEET: THE AMAZINGNESS OF YOU

I know this might feel weird, but describe yourself (focusing on your way of communicating, your style, your tone):

Now, hand this off to a loved one—or call them up and ask them! How do THEY describe you and your style?

List 5 things that make you blissfully happy:

1.

2.

3.

4.

5.

List 5 words or phrases you say all the time:

1.

2.

3.

4.

5.

List 5 qualities that you love (find a list of qualities in the appendixes)

1.

2.

3.

4.

5.

We now have a clear idea of the awesomeness you bring; now let's look at the awesomeness of your thing. As we talk about *your thing,* we're referring to whatever you sell. It might be your retail shop and the experience you provide, or the thing you make by hand and sell online.

I know that *you* know what you make, but it's important to write it down, in detail, so that you'll be able to communicate its awesomeness and make good marketing decisions. When you can communicate its benefits to yourself, here, you'll be able to make it clear to everyone you meet. The fabulousness will shine through brightly on your website. There will be so many times when communicating the benefits of your product will come up (craft show applications, conversations in the coffeeshop, etc.), and you won't have time to prepare. Getting clear *now* means that you'll be clear *then*, when you most need it on the tip of your tongue.

First, **define your thing**. Really spell out what you make and what it includes.

WORKSHEET: WHAT YOU SELL

If you have several product lines, start a different worksheet for each line. Use as many technical terms as you like (e.g., *handspun organic wool from Fiber Farm is handdyed with Procion X dyes using an immersion method*).

Describe what you sell:

What are the qualities of the product? (*e.g., if you sell handmade scarves, what describes the scarves? striped? textural? sophisticated? organic?*)

1.
2.
3.
4.

What it is:

How you make it:

Where those supplies come from:

How it's sold:

How you deliver it:

What's different about how you made it?

When someone else sees it, what's the first thing they comment on?

Look back at what you wrote. What words in your description describe something that's different than what other people do? Circle those words.

Write a paragraph describing your thing, focusing on the traits you circled:

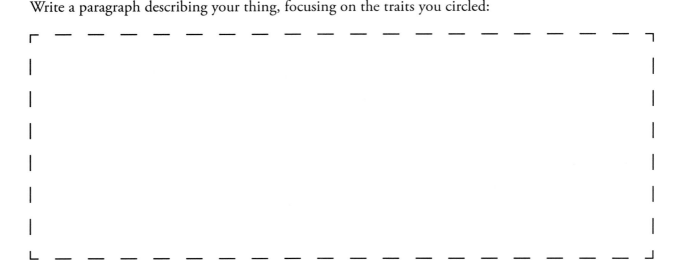

Now that you know the amazingness of you and your thing, we're going to formulate it in a message, but your message has to focus on your customer. We're going to create a message in terms of what your ideal customer wants and needs. While we haven't dug deep into your Right People yet, it's OK to imagine one for the next section.

Just think about it for a second: **Who buys what you sell?**

Maybe they're not buying *your* thing yet, but someone out there is buying something *like* it. Women are buying jewelry. Moms are buying scarves. Families are buying cups.

So, before we go further, think of the kind of person who will want what you sell, even if you have to imagine them as someone else's customer. Knowing what you know about them (that they buy your kind of thing)... what else do you know about them?

Start with the general knowledge (e.g., people who buy earrings have pierced ears) and then get specific (e.g., people who buy bird earrings like birds and have pierced ears). Once you start thinking about your style and your brand, you'll be able to say even more about your ideal customer. If your tone is irreverent and funny, you know they have a sense of humor and aren't too formal. If your tone is sophisticated and high end, you know they value quality and have some disposable income that they aren't afraid to spend on themselves.

Take what you know about them so far, and start to consider what you know about what you make.

FANCY MARKETERS' TALK ABOUT FEATURES VS. BENEFITS

Features = the objective aspects of your Thing. The color, the size, the add-ons. This is what it IS.
Benefits = the subjective awesome of your Thing. What the color will do for the buyer. How the size is handy or delightful or surprising. The way an add-on makes the whole thing more usable. This is what your customer is buying.

The reason we've dug into exactly what is awesome about your thing is that we want to communicate that to your Right People. We've tried to get beyond the features into the benefits.

People buy benefits. They make decisions based on the *benefit* your thing is going to give *them*. The need it's going to fill. The way it makes them *feel*.

People buy to fill a need. Skeezy marketers exploit this by manipulating your feelings so that you believe you *need* their item in order to fill a hole in your life. They manufacture this need and play on your insecurities.

We aren't going to do that. Instead, we're going to explore the needs that your Right People are already feeling and we're going to gently explain how your thing fills their need. We aren't going to manipulate them, nor are we going to promise benefits your thing won't deliver on. (Your thing is so awesome, there's no need to overpromise!)

Focus on them
Your Right People are looking for the thing that is right for them. They love getting to know you; they love seeing your process; they love connecting. But when it's time to hand over their dough, they want to know:

> Is this right for *me*?
> Does it fill my need?
> Does it fulfill my desires?

Not sure how your thing fills a need? Artists and those who create non-functional pieces can get flustered by the fill-a-need thing.

What need does art meet?

WHAT'S A NEED?
There's a theory in psychology that defines human motivation, called the Hierarchy of Needs, by Abraham Maslow. It's a pyramid illustrating what needs motivate human beings.

At the bottom of the hierarchy are physical and safety needs. Your art probably doesn't fill that need. But the very next step up on the needs pyramid are community and a sense of belonging. This is where your art comes in.

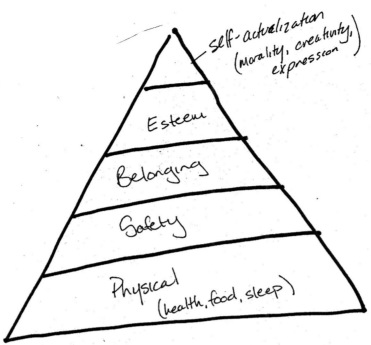

Your thing (and buying it) makes your Right People feel like they belong to a tribe of like-minded people (people who value handmade, and especially people who value your specific aesthetic).

On the next level is esteem and confidence. Your art fills that need because of the feeling it gives the buyer when they purchase it and when they show it off to their friends and get compliments. *I made a great decision. I have fabulous taste.*

The highest level of the pyramid is self-expression and creativity. Of course your art is the physical manifestation of your self-expression, but it can also be a way for your non-making buyers to express themselves. Decorating their home (or themselves) with your thing is a way for them to express their creativity. (We all know that frisson of excitement when you pair the perfect earrings with the top that makes your eyes shine.)

If you paint and sell your artwork, your work can serve as someone else's self-expression. The buyer sees your item and it speaks to them; it expresses something about themselves that they want to express. When they hang your work in their house, it's a statement of who they are and what they value. By buying and displaying your art, they've taken a step to bring more beauty into their life and they've changed their surroundings to reflect their own vision.

Your artwork will also serve a social need. When your buyer has friends over and they see your painting, it gives the buyer a chance to tell a story (your story!) about the artist and the day they bought it. This story is a connection between the buyer and you, and between the buyer and their friends. It helps them define themselves and fit in with other people like them (art-lovers!)

PRICE IS NOT A BENEFIT

When you think about benefits, it's easy to get them mixed up with price... but price is a *feature*, not a *benefit*. Your price communicates the quality and value of what you've created. Although some very high-priced items may be out of some people's reach, a low-priced item communicates low value.

Please remember: You are not competing with Wal-mart.

And not just because you can't (*really, you can't!*) but because your Right People don't want you to be Wal-mart.

They want originality.
Personality.
Specificity.
Personal connection.

Wal-mart provides cheap, mass-produced goods, *cheaply*. You make hand-crafted, high quality, one-of-a-kind goodness to people who are willing to pay for it.

As long as you think of Wal-mart as the competition, you'll spend your time explaining how you're better than them.

But that's a waste of time.

Remember how your English teacher used to say "Show, don't Tell"? Show your personality. Show your originality. Show your you-ness.

And you'll never have to mention "low prices" or "great deals."

Here's a short list of general benefits that you have that Wal-Mart doesn't:

- You are a real person. The buyer gets to interact with a real person. And not just ANY person, a person who MADE the thing they're buying.
- You can provide fabulous, agile customer support.
- You are an artist. People adore supporting artists and the artist community.
- Your thing is one of a kind. The buyer will have something that no one else has.

Of course, you probably know this.

But do your customers know it?
Do you make it ultra-freaking clear that what you make *is valuable*?

HOW WE FIGURE OUT BENEFITS

Start with the list of awesomeness that is your thing (See *Worksheet: What you Sell* on page 25.) Take yourself out of your maker shoes and put yourself in your buyer's shoes. What does each item on your list mean for them?

Some examples

Example 1: If you make yarn from local sheep fleece (feature!) what does that mean for the customer? They will be making an environmentally responsible choice (esteem). They can feel good knowing they're supporting local farmers (belonging). They are part of a bigger circle of sustainable decisions that benefit farmer, animal, spinner, knitter and wearer (sense of belonging).

Example 2: Dryden makes stylish, bold jewelry that generates a lot of compliments. (I know, I have a pair of her earrings and get complimented every time I wear them!)

- I (as the buyer) am delighted to support an artist (belonging + esteem).
- I love being complimented on them (esteem) and telling people the story of buying them (belonging).
- When I pair the earrings with the blue shirt (creativity!) that makes my eyes look extra-blue, I feel most like myself, I feel like I'm in congruence with what I believe (supporing artists), and what I am (blue-eyed, bold)… and that's about as close as a pair of earrings can get to bringing me to the tip-top of the pyramid: self-actualization.

Make it clear.

You should have a good list of the benefits for your buyer of your thing. You are clear about why they want it, but now you have to help your person understand that these benefits are for *them*. You have to help them see your product in their life. In other words, you turn the benefits (this color is happy-making) into something that they can't resist.

The quickest way to get them there is to help them imagine themselves owning it and using it. What will they feel like as they walk down the street? What conversations will they have about it? What will their friends say?

If you feel stuck coming up with your benefits, keep asking "And?" I make bold earrings… *and*? I use local wool… *and*?

> **A note about filling in the next worksheet:** Why, yes, I am asking you to make up stuff about an imaginary person. Some of my students resist this exercise, exclaiming that they don't have enough information to be sure. Or they're worried that they will get it wrong. So just take a deep breath right here. It's OK.
>
> At this point, it's OK to be making it up. It's OK to have one person in mind and learn (*through selling!*) that your Right Person is someone else. It's really OK.

WORKSHEET: BENEFITS AND NEEDS

What are the features of what you make?

How does that translate into benefits for your Right Person?

How does your thing make the buyer feel when she buys it?

How does it make the buyer feel when she uses it?

What desire or want did she have right before she decided to buy it?

How does your thing fill that want?

IMAGINING THE MOST RIGHT PERSON

When I first started dyeing and spinning yarn, I didn't know anyone who knit with hand-dyed, hand-spun yarn. Social media didn't exist, so I didn't have any way of connecting with other hand-spun lovers. Instead, I started with just one person in mind, one knitter whose blog I read (confession: It was Lauren of Lollyknitingaround.com). She didn't knit with a lot of hand-spun yarn, but she cared where yarn came from, so I started sharing that.

- I wrote blog posts about the research I had done on my supplies.
- I wrote about the pains I took to dye in an environmentally-responsible way.
- I told her (in my head it was *her*; publicly, it was just a blog post) what I thought she would love about the yarn.
- I shared patterns she would want to knit.

And then I went looking for some real people. Even if they weren't MY customers, I still needed to find the people who would spend $30 for a skein of yarn. So I went to the fanciest yarn shop in town and offered to dye some "exclusive colorways" for the shop. The owner was thrilled and asked me if I wanted to work there a few hours a week. Even though I had a more-than-full-time job (managing a paint-your-own-pottery studio), I jumped at it.

My work in that yarn shop introduced me to the people who would become my first customers. They spent more than $30 on a skein of yarn. Unlike Lauren, they were *beginner* knitters and they wanted to knit in order to use the yarn they fell in love with. They wanted simple patterns that would just let them enjoy the texture and color of the yarn.

So then I started answering *their* questions on my blog. I started using the terms they searched for in my site. I provided them with simple pattern ideas.

As I started selling online, I met even more customers who liked how I seemed to be talking right to them. They were very similar to the women I met at the yarn shop, so I kept focusing on them.

Now when I write, I keep one particularly wonderful customer in mind (Minnie) and write everything for her. I use my newsletter software to see what she and other subscribers click on most, which email subject headers they open, and what yarns they buy… so not only am I talking to them, I'm also using what they're telling me to talk to them more effectively.

Keep going until you get to emotional reaction point, for the buyer.

Your thing does fulfill a need or desire, for someone. You *doing your thing* will touch, reach, and inspire someone else.

And that someone else needs you to explain how your thing is going to touch or reach or inspire them. In fact, they want you to explain it to them.

Learning to recognize the benefits of your thing and communicating it your customers, helps them know your thing is right for them (or not).

You can also tell them the story behind making your thing (not the technical aspect, but the inspiration). When you made it, how did you imagine them using it?

Stop describing why *you* like it as a technician (e.g., mono-print using blah-blah grade ink) and start painting the vision of your product in their life. Take all of the emotional and social ties that *you* feel toward the item and mirror that for the customer. For example, you love the bright color because it makes you happy. Describe how happy it will make them. In what situation? What will they experience?

As my friend Catherine Caine likes to say: **People are selfish.**

They may adore you, but they *really* want information that makes them feel good and makes them look good. They want a story to share with others; they want to feel smart and cute and clever for having bought what you made. Connecting with you, caring about you, is part of this. It makes them feel good or generous or part of something bigger. Or smart or clever or unique. But you have to help them see that, you have to paint that picture for them on your website, in your descriptions, in your conversations.

BOIL IT ALL DOWN

Let's take everything you've learned in this chapter and boil it back down to that simple message: "I sell this and you should care because…." Take your answers from this chapter's worksheets and use them to answer the following worksheet.

WORKSHEET: BOIL IT DOWN

Using all the other worksheets in this chapter, answer the following questions using just one sentence.

Who are you? What makes you qualified or weird or noteworthy?

What do you sell?

What makes it unique?

What are the benefits for the buyer?

What are the qualities of your brand?

Now condense it even further. Combine it all into a coherent, declarative sentence or two.

Some examples:
I care passionately about small farms and sustainable fiber, so I spin and dye eco-friendly, fair trade yarn in colors and textures that make you happy.

What you put on your body is just as important as what you put into it. I make all-natural, quality bath and body products, from only the best ingredients—crap-free, guaranteed.

I'm a sarcastic, geeky fangirl, so I draw nerdy cartoons of the stuff I love, and use them to make the sort of greeting cards your mother warned you about.

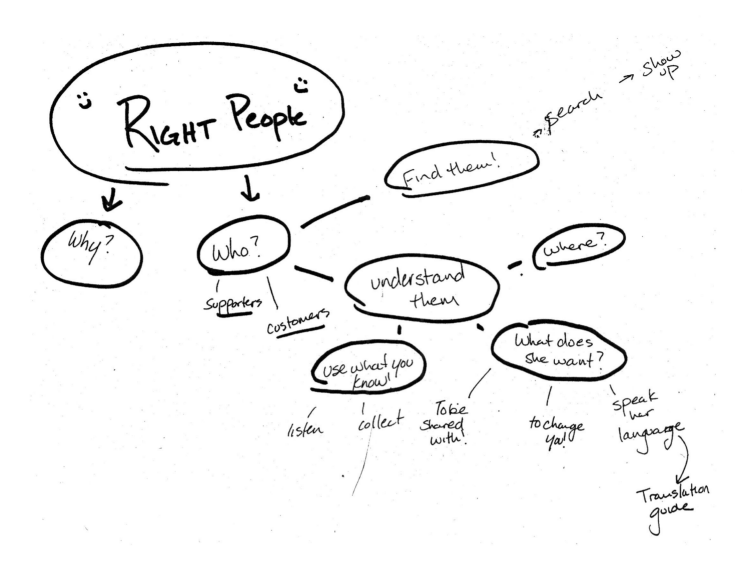

CHAPTER 3: RIGHT PEOPLE

Now that you have your message, you're ready to think about **sharing it.**

We all know that creating is deeply enriching for you. It gives you expression, freedom, a place in the world. The *making* is about you. The *selling*, the *sharing*, needs to be all about them.

Your Right People.[†]

WHO ARE RIGHT PEOPLE?

Your Right People are the people who are your ideal customers, the people who will support you and share your thing and celebrate with you. The people who will be delighted when you share your true you-ness in your work.

These might not be people with the most money. Or the most power. Or the people who will tell you what to change.

Your Right People may change as you change, but the fact is: you will always have Right People. You can sell offensive, ridiculous, or downright crazy stuff and it will be just perfect for the Right People. You never don't have Right People, they just might not have *found* you yet.

The only way to create something that doesn't have a Right Person is to create something bland, generic, or vague. When you create things that don't come from your own strengths and passion (your you-ness!), you'll have a hard time finding your Right People… because no one gets excited about mediocrity.

Some of these Right People will *buy* your thing and some will simply *support* your thing. Supporters are important. They include mentors, partners, fellow makers, and people who like what you make even though it's not for them. They can make connections for you, spread the word, and even encourage you in dark times. Depending on where you are in your business, you may want to spend more or less time building up your supporters. But in general, you want to spend more time reaching out to potential customers, those Right People who actually *want* your thing in their life, than to fellow crafters, cheerleaders, and mentors (who may be your consumers or readers.)

From here on out when we talk about Right People, we mean **customers**, those people who are willing to spend money on what you make. Just keep in mind that as you work to attract and delight customers you will also be collecting supporters along the way.

The most common question I get from crafters is, "Should I use (fill in the blank with a tool)?"

[†] *thanks to Havi, of FluentSelf.com for making up this perfect phrase, and for being a beautiful demonstration of non-icky marketing.*

Blogging, Twitter, Facebook, Myspace, Pinterest, and all the things that haven't been invented yet—how do you know what you should use?
The answer is simple: do your Right People use that?

So before we talk about where to share your message, let's talk about who you're sharing that message with.

- Where are they?
- What are they using?
- How do they want to find out about your thing?
- What do they already know about your thing?

No matter who your Right People are, you will definitely want a base of operations (either your website or your physical retail/studio space), a space where your Right Person will come and feel welcomed and get comfortable buying what you sell.

WHY ALL THE FOCUS ON RIGHT PEOPLE?

Because your Right People will shape your message. They will determine where you do your marketing, what you share, and how you share it. They will help you focus your marketing efforts and direct your path.

If you develop a circle of Right People and you work to keep them happy, it's the only marketing you'll ever have to do.

If you attract the Right People while doing your own thing, you can build exactly the kind of business you love, one that's full of your favorite things, without worrying about whether or not they'll stick around.

You simply do your thing—and your Right People will be there cheering and buying.

Without a focus on your Right People your business may be:

- **Unfocused:** Which way should I go next? What should I make?
- **Uncertain:** Will this sell? Where should I advertise?
- **Insecure:** Will people like it? Is it worthless? Will anyone ever buy?

Focusing on your Right People can prevent (or reverse) all that.

When you're talking to your Right People, you can be yourself—because that spark of YOU is what spoke to the people in the first place. It's why they are here, checking out your thing.

When you talk to your Right People, you know what to do next—they'll tell you what they want either directly (*I want yellow!*) or indirectly (yellow sells out quickly).

When you share your thing with the Right People, you'll make sales—they will feel a sense of kinship or a recognition of awesomeness and it will *click*. (*Yes, this is for me!*)

It's not about manipulation, convincing, or cajoling. In fact, it's the opposite! When you speak to your Right People, you don't have to persuade them that your thing is right. They will feel it.

Now that I've convinced you to figure out your Right People, let's jump right into it. Fill out the following worksheet!

UNDERSTANDING RIGHT PEOPLE

For most of us, what we make is a reflection of us. The personality of our brand is an aspect of our own personality. This is great (and helps you maintain a cohesive voice) but it can also distract us when thinking about Right People. It's easy to imagine our Right Person is just like us. Or, if we sell something expensive, that they're nothing like us and that we don't understand them at all.

So let's see your Right Person for who she really is:

1. You *make* your thing, and while your Right Person might be a lot like you, she does *not* make your thing (or else, why would she buy it?).
2. Your Right Person probably has more disposable income than you do.
3. Your Right Person, while valuing the handmade, doesn't understand the value of it: the time you took, the process, the creativity. It's up to you to explain it in a way that enthralls her.
4. Your Right Person, even if she has way more money than you and is not at all crafty, still values what you value. She's also working from the same desires, wants, and needs.
5. Your Right Person is just as smart as you. She can sense your tone and pick up on your mood when you write to her. Don't lie, don't bend the truth, and don't condescend to her.

Now that you know all this, is there anything you need to change in your description of your Right Person?

WORKSHEET: THE RIGHT PERSON

Male or Female?

Age:

Lifestyle/location/peer group:

Give her a name:

Say something insanely specific about her here:

What does she read?

What does she watch?

Does she listen to podcasts? If so, which ones?

Is she on Twitter? If so, what's she talking about?

Is she super-active in Facebook groups? If so, which ones?

Where does she shop?

How does she decide WHAT to buy?

What does she do for fun?

What else?

We dove right in, because you *do know*. If you're at all familiar with what you create and sell, then you know what people use it for. You know what your Right Person is going to love about it (hint: it's in your What I Sell worksheet on page 25). If you've sold anything already, you can use what you know about your past customers to fill in the worksheet.

If you truly can't think of a person who would need this product, then it's likely that you think no one wants what you make. But we're not yet to the point of getting people to buy your thing, we're just talking about people who buy things *like yours*—the general category. Do you make cards? Then we're talking about people who buy cards. Do you make scarves? Then people who wear scarves. Do you make yarn? Then people who use yarn.

If you truly, truly can not imagine this person, ask yourself this: is there any store, anywhere in the world that carries your product category? (I'm sure there is!)

Who shops there?

There you go! *That* is the Right Person to start with!

Now we're going to start imagining her journey. How does your Right Person end up on your doorstep (or website)? How does she decide she wants what you sell? Where does your product fit into her life and her day?

WORKSHEET: WHERE IS YOUR RIGHT PERSON?

_____ JUST decided she needs a _____
(Fill in name with your Right Person.) (Fill in with what you make.)

Yay!

What happened right before this story started?

What does she do next?

If she does that, will she find you?

Where does she go to look? List 3 places, sites or search terms.

How can you be THERE where she's looking? (*List at least ten ways for each place—get crazy!*)

HOW RIGHT PEOPLE CHANGED MY BUSINESS

I'd like to share what happened in my business when I started applying the concept of Right People to my work. It started when my teacher and friend Havi said:

Everyone has Right People and
Your Right People are Right if they love what you do. That's the only requirement.

And I wondered, "what would this look like *if I really believed it?*" If these people love what I make, then I should make something truly ME.

Instead of worrying about the trends or what other yarnies were doing, I started focusing on yarn that I really love. Textures, colors, styles. My love of my work grew and I created a line of yarns that really went together. I began to develop a look for Blonde Chicken Boutique.

If there are people who love what I make, then I should be talking to THEM. Instead of spending money reaching tons of new people, I turned to my current people. How can I serve them better? For starters, I ask them. I create products they want (the Learn to Knit Kit was inspired by people who loved my yarn but didn't knit) and I keep them up to date (with a customers-only newsletter and a bi-weekly Yarn-Love Note).

My Right People love my thing, so why worry about those who don't?

When I realized that I don't have to appeal to everyone or make everyone happy, I knew I could focus on doing what I do best and serving the people who are already happy. My happy, delighted Right People are the best advertising I could ever want. If I make it easy for them to share my stuff, they will spread the word to more Right People.

The more I thought about Right People, I realized I was actually thinking about **marketing**.

But instead of asking "How do I tell people about my thing" (like many crafters do) or "How do I tell my target market of 30-year-old college graduates who make $40,000 per year who knit about my thing" (like marketers do), I'm asking, "Who are my Right People already? What do they love? What could I do to make them happier?"

This changed every part of my marketing. The result? My time is spent working with people I love, instead of stressing over finding more people. My people are happy and tell their friends. My sales (online, in person at craft shows, and in yarn shops) have greatly increased. But best of all, *I'm doing what I actually love.*

WHAT WOULD YOUR BUSINESS LOOK LIKE IF YOU ONLY FOCUSED ON YOUR RIGHT PEOPLE?

SPEAK HER LANGUAGE

Now that you have a picture of your Right People, you probably want to jump right into finding them, but before you do, let's think about how to make sure *they* know that they are your Right People. Specifically, how will they know that your thing is what they want to buy?

The simplest answer is: **you'll tell them**. Even better, you'll tell them why they want your thing in language that makes sense to them.

Let's look back at the picture you have of your Right People. Why do they buy what you sell? What are they looking for?

Now look at what you make. How does it meet their needs? How is it what they're looking for? This comes back to features and benefits. The features are the **aspects** of your product, while the benefits are what actually **affect** the buyer. Your buyer wants to know what this thing is going to do for them and how they'll feel when they own it. We did this a bit in the last chapter, but now we're going to take it one step further and make a full translation guide for your communication.

A **translation guide** will help you take what you want to say about the product and translate it into what your Right Person wants to hear about the product. This guide helps you describe the features, while making the benefits crystal clear. It also helps you bridge the gap between how you think about your product and how your buyer thinks about it.

To create your own personal translation guide, you're going to have to jump back and forth between your perspective as the maker and your buyer's perspective. I find it easiest to think in maker mode, then take a little break and come back in buyer mode.

WORKSHEET: TRANSLATION GUIDE

For this worksheet, write your answers on the left side, and then come back later and fill out the right side. Before you fill out that right side, get in the mindframe of your right buyer. How do you do that? If you've already made sales, go back and read comments and emails from your buyers. Notice the words they use to describe what they love or why they bought from you. Copy and paste their answers right into your worksheet—they're pure gold!

If you haven't made sales yet, that's OK! We're going to play make believe. Using the previous worksheets, imagine your Right Person. Give her a name, an income level, a job, a family (whatever that might look like for her—two cats? 12 kids?).

Now, she wants what you sell because…? What does she say upon finding it? With her firmly in mind, go through and answer the right side of this worksheet.

My answers, as the maker	Her answers, as the buyer
Start with how you make it. Describe the process (and what's unique about the way *you* do it vs. the way other people might do it). 1. 2. 3. 4.	What does this give the buyer? 1. 2. 3. 4.

My answers, as the maker	Her answers, as the buyer
OK, now branch out into aspects of the product. What's included? What does it look like?	Why does this matter to the buyer?
1.	1.
2.	2.
3.	3.
4.	4.
Does your product come with options (color, size, etc.)? List them here.	What do these options mean for the buyer?
1.	1.
2.	2.
3.	3.
4.	4.

HOW TO USE THE TRANSLATION GUIDE

This translation guide can help you in every conversation you have about your product. From conversations in craft show booths, to your product descriptions, to your blog posts. Any time you want to describe a product, use words and phrases found on the right side of this document. When you write your home page, take your pictures or apply for a craft show, use the translation guide.

FINDING YOUR RIGHT PEOPLE

OK, now that you know how to talk to your Right People, it's time to go out and find them! We're going to talk more about starting conversations online and offline in coming chapters, but for now, let's think about how you will find your people.

It all starts with the worksheets you've filled out about your Right People. Where are they? What do they read? Where do they hang out online? The answers to these questions tell you where to find your Right People. Once you know where they are, you want to show up there. That means different things for different populations, so let's look at some examples.

For online sites (like Twitter, Facebook groups, etc.) you'll want to start with a search. Don't just search for what you sell, search for what else your people are talking about. People who buy jewelry might be talking about fashion (or a show about fashion). Moms who buy onesies will likely be talking about kids, breastfeeding, and diaper changes. Knitters will be talking about yarn and specific projects. You can use search.twitter.com to find users tweeting about these subjects and you can use Google's blog search to find bloggers who blog about these topics. Showing up in these spots means creating an account—with a profile that links back to your site—and then starting conversations, listening, and becoming a virtual citizen of the groups that your people belong to.

For offline spots, it's easier—you physically show up where you're Right People are. If it's moms, you go to Mommy+Me groups (it probably helps if you have a baby of your own to bring with you). If it's fashion-minded jewelry buyers, you get your goods into their favorite shops. If it's knitters, start a knitting group and go to the conventions.

Showing up in the right spot can even be as simple as showing up in a store where your Right Person shops. Amy started selling her sci-fi-inspired cards to a local comic book shop. One day, a woman who worked at a fantasy game company came into the shop and spotted the cards. The cards were so perfect for her and her company that she commissioned 1,000 cards from Amy to use as the company's Christmas cards!

This is why it's important to know who your Right People are: it will help you focus your decisions. For example, if you sell knitted blankets, getting published in a knitting magazine would not reach your Right People… because your Right People aren't knitters, they are buyers-of-knitting.

Now let's imagine that you've met some Right People. You've made sales and you're getting a clearer and clearer idea of who your people are.

Now what?

Your Right People search-and-rescue mission isn't over. In fact, it's just begun. The more you know about your Right People, the more you can focus on making them happy. How do you make them happy?

GIVE YOUR PEOPLE WHAT THEY WANT

Your Right People want you to talk to them.
Your Right People want you to talk *like* them.
Your Right People want to change your business.

LET RIGHT PEOPLE CHANGE YOU
- Your Right People love you, and if asked, would say that they *don't* want to change anything about you. And while they might believe that, the truth is, your Right People can radically transform your business—in the best way possible.
- Your Right People can bring you more Right People (and more sales means a different scale of business).
- Your Right People can introduce you to people who can change your business (retail stores, craft show organizers, editors, producers, movers and shakers).
- Your Right People can also change your business by asking questions—if you listen to them.
- Your Right People will buy your thing, encourage you, and gush about you. They'll also complain, coax, and ask for something new. They might comment about the time it took their package to arrive. They might say, "*Boy, I really wish you had this in green.*" It's easy to ignore these small comments and let them get buried in your inbox.

But please don't!

After weeks (months?) of looking for your Right People, of listening in on them, of trying to guess what they want and how they talk—you've got someone real! You finally have a live person giving you feedback… so celebrate!

Collect their comments and once a week (or once a day) sort through them and find out what you can do (and what you can't). Reply to the people who wrote and let them know how you're using their feedback to transform your business. Tell them that you now carry green because they asked for it. Tell them that you now ship three times a week instead of one because they wanted it.

BE OPEN TO HAVING YOUR VISION FOR YOUR RIGHT PERSON CHANGED
You might have started the worksheets in this book with one person in your mind. But as you've made sales, visited craft shows, and talked to shop owners, you've learned that a whole other kind of buyer is buying.

This is a good thing.

It means that while you might have been wrong, you have the chance to be right. Learn as much as you can about your real Right Person. Start asking her questions. Listen to the language she uses. Pay attention to why she says she buys. Notice all the ways she is like what you imagined and all the ways she isn't. Perhaps she values what you thought she did, but she's just a bit older (or younger). Perhaps she makes much more money than you imagined and wants a new, higher-end collection.

YOUR RIGHT PEOPLE WANT YOU TO TALK TO THEM

Your people want you to talk directly to them. They want to know that you get them and that you know them. They want you to use the language they use. They want you to describe the benefits that appeal to them. They want you to help them make the right decision and buy the perfect gift. Show them you get them by continuing to tweak your descriptions and your writing (blog posts, emails, tweets) to reflect what they tell you is most important to them.

YOUR RIGHT PEOPLE WANT YOU TO TALK TO THEM

They want to hear from you. Not just when they remember to visit your website or blog, but on a regular basis. They want to remember that they loved you. They want to know you're thinking of them. So don't worry that you're being too sales-y—just go on and send them an email. Send one to a past customer where you check in on her, or send an email to your newsletter list just filling them in on what's happening.

Give your Truly Right People (your past customers) special treatment and give them rewards for sticking with you—free shipping, $5 off, or just the option to buy something no one else can buy. Before you offer a new customer a discount, a special, or an incentive, ask yourself if your past customers would like it. What can you do to make your past customers delightfully happy?

Say thank you!
Do I need to say more here?

The best thing you can do with your Right People is to thank them, early and often. Thank them after each purchase, thank them in the package (in the form of a real, handwritten thank-you note), thank them when they refer someone else to you, thank them for telling their friends about your craft show. Thank them for linking to your blog post.

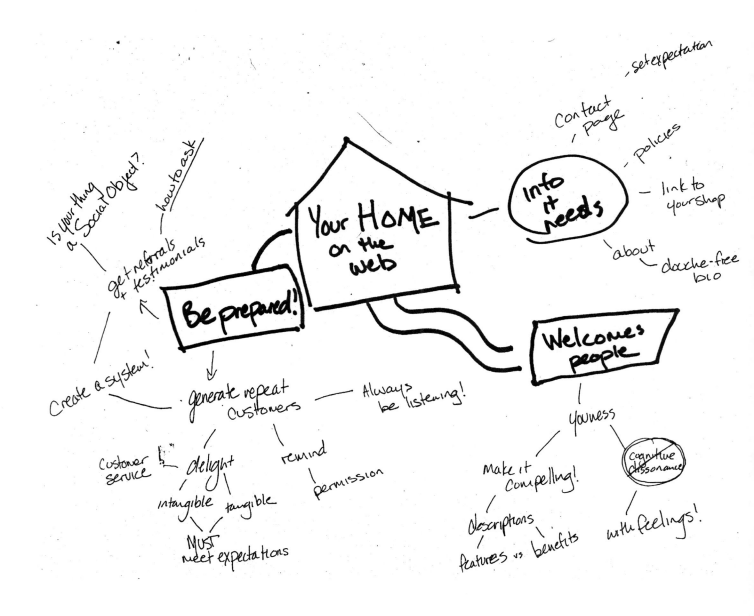

CHAPTER 4: BUILDING YOUR HOME

Now we get into sharing your thing: putting it online and in front of people. But before you go out and start inviting people to your party, you want to make sure your home is in order. Your business's home is your website. (If you have a retail shop, this chapter applies to both your website and your physical shop.) It's where you invite everyone. It's where you do all your planning.

- If you want to buy an ad, you first set up the page on your site to which the ad will point.
- If you are active on social media, your profile links back to your website.
- If you go to craft shows, everything you hand out (business cards, product tags, flyers) includes links back to your site.

Your home turns Right People into customers.

It's a space that's completely *you*, where your Right People won't get distracted and go someplace else. (This is why you probably don't want to sell advertisements on your sidebar… they encourage people to click away.)

If you don't have a home that turns people into customers, then all of your marketing activities will be wasted. Getting people to your site won't do a lot of good if the site doesn't turn them into customers. Your website is at the heart of turning strangers into buyers. It might entice them first into becoming consumers (readers and followers), but it's final goal is to turn them into buyers.

It does this magic act in a few ways:
- It **welcomes them** into the universe of your business.
- It **gives them all the information** they need to make an informed decision.
- It **seduces them** to come closer, learn more, and act.

After your site is effective, your home-building isn't quite done yet. You also want to have a few more systems in place to support the customers after they buy. This will ensure that each customer is delighted and that you're ready to invite them to become a *repeat* customer and refer your work to others.

Let's start by making your home ready for the party, then we'll work on delighting the customer and bringing them (and their friends) back for more.

YOUR WEBSITE WELCOMES PEOPLE INTO YOUR UNIVERSE

Your website, your home, is the place people come to find out more about you and your product. The experience they have on the site directly impacts how they feel about you and determines if they're comfortable buying from you. It's not enough for them to know you're selling something; they also have to feel comfortable and reassured that you're a real person, worthy of their trust. Over time, your site also reaffirms the specific personality of your business. (This personality is called your **brand**.) To do this, you make the site cohesively filled with you-ness. Yep, we're back to the worksheets you filled out in Chapter 1.

To make sure you're Right People know they're in the right place—to make them feel cozy and welcome—your site needs to be clearly, uniquely *yours.*

All this talk about your you-ness and applying it to your site might not seem like real marketing—I mean, of course you know how to be yourself! But there is a reason we keep coming back to your message and your style: we're trying to avoid *cognitive dissonance.*

Cognitive dissonance is that discomfort you feel when something doesn't match up with your expectations. It's when you have one idea or concept in mind, and then you're surprised when what you find doesn't match that. This cognitive dissonance happens a lot online, when a person's site doesn't match their tone. Or their grammatical mistakes don't match their prices. Or their photographs don't match their descriptions. It's easy to create cognitive dissonance because, in the beginning, our online skills (or photography or writing) might not match up with our real-world personality and brand. If you feel uncomfortable online (or with writing), you might behave stiffly or more formally than you usually would.

Our reaction to cognitive dissonance is avoidance. We try not to experience it, so when we encounter it online, we click away.

That's why it's important, as sellers and creators of an online world, to pay attention to the cohesiveness of your brand. We don't want people to click away. We don't want our potential buyers to feel uncomfortable. In everything we put online, we want to be consistent so that we create comfort and safety for our buyers.

ONCE MORE, WITH FEELING

Take a look at your site: does it reflect what you discovered in Chapter 1? Does the person you described on the Right People worksheet feel comfortable here? Go back to your list of benefits (on page 45) and think about what your Right Person is really looking for. Is it comfort? Ease? Color? Excitement? That is how your site should make you—and her—feel.

Your site is your first opportunity for your Right Person to *feel* how your item will make her feel. It's a sample of what working with you and living with your thing will be like.

- If you sell exciting, cutting-edge art installations, your site will be electrifying, exciting, and daring. They'll feel a little rush of adrenaline just by being on your site.
- If you sell comfy, snuggly blankets, your site will make them feel comfortable, comforted, and warmed.
- If you sell stylish jewelry, your site will make them feel hip, pretty, and clever.

WORKSHEET: HOW DO YOU WANT YOUR CUSTOMER TO FEEL?

When your product is *exactly* what your customer wants, how does it make her feel ?

How can your site reflect that?

What can you include in your site to generate those feelings?
(words, colors, stories, pictures)

WORKSHEET: HOW OTHER SITES MAKE ME FEEL

How a site makes you feel is highly subjective of course, but the best way to learn is to visit sites and notice how they make you feel. Pull up one of your favorite sites on your browser (pick one from a big company, one that has paid for professional branding).

Take note of what this site makes you feel in the first five seconds.

Notice the:

- layout

- colors

- pictures

- words + tone

Now go looking for a site that makes you feel the way you want your Right People to feel.

Take note of what this sites make you feel in the first five seconds.

Notice the:

- layout

- colors

- pictures

- words + tone

Remember: you're not going to make a site *like* someone else's; you're going to take these elements and add your you-ness—your colors, your vocabulary and your strengths. When putting together your site for the first time (or just reviewing it to make sure it has what your people need), it's helpful to write out each page, before you try to put it online. Use the following worksheet to flesh out your site.

WORKSHEET: YOUR WEBSITE

What do you want visitors to your site to do?

How can you make this easy and obvious?

Is there information they need to have before they buy?

What do you want your site to say about your company?

What will the buyer want to know about your company?

Does your site reflect the benefits you've listed in your Right People worksheet?

Where?

Could you be more specific about the benefits (*hint: YES*)? Where?

What other information could give you the buyer?

Where will you put it?
(e.g., item description, policies page, in a blog post)

Your site is now cohesive and full of information that your buyer needs. The last piece of the puzzle: *is it compelling?*

YOUR WEBSITE GIVES ALL THE INFORMATION THEY NEED

In order to buy something, you need to know it's for sale, feel comfortable buying it, and know everything you need to know (i.e., not have any remaining questions). This is where the pages of your website and the hard facts come in handy. Your buyer expects to be able to find a few things on your site.

What your website needs
- an about page
- a clear link to how they buy your thing, right there on the homepage
- info about shipping + policies
- a way to contact you (whichever format you respond to most quickly)

Before we get started on what can go on these pages, take a moment to think about what your site is going to **do**. It's doing all the heavy lifting in a web-based business: it's both introducing strangers to your brand and turning visitors into customers. There will be a lot of information on the site, and it's easy to get distracted by getting it all out there, and lose site of the priorities.

If the priority of your site is to sell your products, then make sure that's front and center. You absolutely need everything else to make the visitor feel comfortable buying, but don't let your priority get buried.

About Page
Ah, the dreaded about page! If you've ever tried to write a bio (or an artist statement, or even a cover letter on a resume), you're familiar with the particular agony of trying to write about yourself. (See page 51 for douche-free bio tips.) So first, give yourself permission to not be perfect the first time. In fact, just count on changing it every six months. In your first draft, try to include the information about you that pertains to what you're doing (or is just hilarious—a French major turned yarn maker?). As you edit the page, start to turn it into a story. Where's the turning point? What changed your life and created this business? Even better, bring the customer into it! How have they (your buyers) changed your life, your business, your vision? If your business was a fairy tale, who's the princess? Who's the trusty steed? Who's the evil stepmother?

And the last thing you might want to include is a bit about why YOU are uniquely qualified to do what you do. But be careful here! No one wants a resumé—not even the people who work in HR. Trust me, I used to be one of them.

A Link to Your Shop
This is self-explanatory: make it super clear what you sell and how they can give you money for it! Whether you've got a mini-shop in your sidebar or a big SHOP button in top navigation, this needs to be so obvious that it doesn't take a stranger longer than five seconds to find out how they can buy what you're selling.

16 QUESTIONS TO HELP YOU WRITE A DOUCHE-FREE BIO
by Kelly Parkinson

Are you trying to write your own bio? Then you've probably discovered how hard it is to give your bio a personal touch—without it sounding like a *personals* ad—and while still making prospects feel like they're in good, competent, professional hands.

Whether I'm writing my own bio or someone else's, I find bios the most extraordinarily difficult kind of copy to write. How many of us compress our lives into 200 words or less in real-life conversation? Only the most annoying ones, that's who. Bio-speak has practically developed into its own language. Spend an afternoon reading LinkedIn profiles and you'll become a bio-speak master. "Boring is better" seems to be the prevailing attitude.

Here's an example of bio-speak at its worst:

Jane Madison is an accomplished, seasoned consultant and thought leader with 23 years experience creating top-line and bottom-line results for Fortune-1 companies. That's right—she only works with Fortune's number one company in any given year, producing millions of dollars in revenue. It's unclear whether the beneficiary of this revenue is her or her clients. She's pretty sure it's her clients, although she does live in an exclusive Woodside neighborhood with her husband and their five pedigree horses. She has a BS in Advanced Psychographic Analytics from Harvard University where she made the Dean's List for five years in a row. Although she graduated in a record two years, she remained on the Dean's List for a subsequent three years because of the vast influence her term papers had on the academic world as a whole.

OK, I made this up. But let's assume you want your bio to sound a bit less douche-y than that. Wouldn't it be nice to have a bio that sounded like an actual person wrote it—rather than the bizarro, corporate version of you?

THE FOLLOWING 16 QUESTIONS ARE DESIGNED TO HELP YOU PRODUCE THE RAW INGREDIENTS TO WRITE BIOS THAT PEOPLE DON'T HATE READING.

But before you dig in, please read these instructions:

1. **Set a timer for 26 minutes.** This is very important. Do not skip this step! If you're a Level-9 Procrastinator like me, you'll never start this exercise if you don't give yourself permission to do it quickly. This doesn't have to become a three-hour, story-of-my-life writing intervention. (Unless you want it to.)
2. **Answer the questions in a rambling, conversational style.** You might even write them in the body of an email that you pretend to send to a friend. Don't worry

about perfect sentences. This exercise is not designed to help you craft your bio. It's simply meant to help you dig up all the good, fresh stuff buried in your brain, which you can *then* use to craft your bio. If you hate writing and are better at thinking on your feet, then speak your answers into a recorder or iPhone and transcribe them.

Now you're ready to go. Here are 16 questions to get you started and to keep you from writing a bio-speak bio.

1. How did you arrive at running this business? What path brought you here?

2. What are you known for professionally? What do you have a knack for?

3. What's the one problem you are best at solving for your clients? What do your ideal clients say about you?

4. Who have you worked with in the past? And what have you done for them?

5. What are you most passionate about professionally? What most excites you about your work and the contribution you can make?

6. What are you passionate about personally? What do you really enjoy? What can't you stop talking about?

7. Where can we find you when you're not working? What's your favorite way to spend a weekend or a Sunday afternoon?

8. How long have you been doing what you do?

9. Where did you grow up and why aren't you there now?

10. Any volunteer activities you're crazy about?

11. Any nonprofits you love, and why?

12. Any awards or medals, or even medallions? Personal okay, too.

13. What would be impossible for you to give up?

14. Why would someone not want to work with you?

15. How do you want to be remembered?

16. Anything else you'd like to tell people about yourself?

Let your answers to these questions sit for a while. Then bold the answers that seem interesting, unexpected, insightful, profound, or just plain feel uniquely you.

Shipping + Policies

This doesn't need be a separate page or in the main navigation. You can put this on your Shop page or link to it from your Shop page or your About page. Just make it easy to find. Link to it whenever anyone asks you a question (instead of just answering their one question), because it will keep things clear and easy.

Contact

Most people are going to look for a page that says "Contact" so don't try to be clever here. Be sure to include the ways you want to be contacted and *when they can expect to hear from you.*

These pages are just the most obvious things you want to have on your site. But what else needs to be in place before you start bringing people into your living room?

HOW TO MAKE IT COMPELLING

Everything up until now has focused on the big picture of your website. But the bulk of your day-to-day time is really spent on the individual products: making them, posting them for sale, and trying to describe them. While it's vital for the descriptions to reflect your brand (use the previous worksheets!), your description also needs to go one step further and actually be *compelling.*

What we've done so far is create a welcoming space filled with the information a buyer needs. It's like walking into a store (*one that feels comfortable and friendly and like me*) and seeing a shirt on the rack. I can check its label (*yep, my size*), what it looks like (*yep, pretty*) and in theory, I have all the information I need to take it to the cash register. But there's one more step, right? Every one of us tries on the shirt. Or at the very least, I hold it up to myself. Is it *really* the right size? Does it look right with these jeans?

When your customer is shopping online, she can't hold the shirt up to her. She can't feel how smooth the silk is or how cozy the wool is. Your job in the descriptions—and in all of the words on your site—is to help her imagine trying it on.

We talked about this in Chapter 2 when you developed your message. Remember features vs. benefits? They help you develop your overall message (*I make this and this is why you'll love it*), but they also inform every other bit of writing you do.

You want to describe the benefits and help your Right Person picture herself "trying on" your product anytime you ask her to buy. Every product description should help her imagine herself wearing (or living with) the item. Your descriptions paint the picture of the item in her life. Your descriptions will be effective when you talk about the benefits she cares about, in the language she uses.

Let's take the benefits worksheet from Chapter 2 and apply it to each individual product:
*   What are the features of this item?

- How does that translate into a benefit?
- What does your customer want this product to do (both tangibly and intangibly)?
- What about this product will completely delight—and maybe surprise—her?

Your site is the home you invite everyone back to. It's the hub of everything else you do to share your thing with the world. While you want to get your home in order before you start inviting people into it, keep in mind that as you learn more about your business and your Right People, your home will continue to change. You may want to revisit this chapter every six months or so and look at your site from the perspective of one of the customers you know really well (and like). In fact, you can ask a trusted customer (or friend, just make sure it's someone who is a Right Person for your thing), to give you feedback on your site. Ask specific questions and remember that YOU are the final word; you get to decide what you change and what you keep.

Now that your home is ready to invite people into, let's make sure the rest of your business is ready for those buyers. You want to have these pieces in place before you start inviting people back to your place, so that when you get your first customer, *you know what to do with them.* After they place an order, your job is to get their purchase into their hands, and to make them so deliriously happy that they want to come back (again and again). In other words, you want to turn them from a one-time customer into a repeat customer.

REPEAT CUSTOMERS

Customers becomes regulars when they are delighted by their purchases and they *remember* that they were delighted. The first step is to **delight them** when they first buy from you. Delight encompasses all of the tangible and intangible aspects of the experience. Helping customers *remember* their delightful experience involves getting their **permission**, **connecting** with them again, and then **reminding** them of what they like about your product. In this section, we'll cover both aspects of delighting and reminding your customer.

DELIGHT

Even if you haven't made a single sale yet, now that you have your sales-making machine set up, you want to think about what you'll do after you make the sale.

That is, after you're finished jumping for joy and celebrating and calling all your friends.

Now, what? Obviously, you need to fulfill the order. This can be as simple as sticking your thing in an envelope and dropping it in the mail.

Or, this can be *another opportunity to share the awesomeness of your thing.*

Yes, they *bought your thing,* so you've convinced them—up until now—that it's worth it… but you're not done yet. The buyer is waiting for your glorious thing, hoping that it is, in fact, glorious. But if they bought it online, they don't really know. They've put a lot of trust and belief in you and your ability to deliver what you promised.

This is your chance to shine. This is your chance to delight. This is a chance to confirm everything they had hoped and to reinforce all the branding on your site. This is a chance to deliver your message again, in a new form.

Think of what you want the buyer to experience when they open the package. How do you want them to feel? What do you want to them to think?

How will you delight your customer?

You create an experience that both meets their expectations and reminds them why they bought from you in the first place. The tangible and intangible aspects form a cohesive identity. The entire experience is smooth, clear, and reaffirming.

Delight is made up of both the tangible and intangible.

The tangible aspects of your product include the physical product, the wrapping, the labels, and anything else you include in your package. Everything you say to them during the transaction is a tangible aspect of your brand. From the "thank you!" page after they submit payment to the email you send confirming the shipping date.

The intangible aspects are, well… hard to quantify. The most obvious question your customers will be asking themselves is: *Is this exactly what I expected?*

What they expected includes the product itself, the time it took to arrive, and the way it's packaged. It includes the product and the packaging, the voice and the experience. Your package reflects your brand, and everything included will reflect your voice and your you-ness.

MEETING EXPECTATIONS

It's not particularly glamorous, but it can't be skipped. In an effort to make everything pretty and stylized and branded, many crafters forget that their first responsibility is to provide *exactly* what the customer expects. This means:

- The item is exactly what they ordered (color, size, amount).
- The item ships on time.
- You communicate the ship date, estimated shipping time, and the tracking number (if applicable).
- Your communication is friendly, polite, and grateful (not grovelling, just appreciative).

Before you shrug off the above, take a minute and look at your business. Do you have a system set up to meet expectations? Do you have a system for thanking the customer for the order, printing the shipping label, notifying the customer of shipping date and time, and then packing up the order and getting it to the post office?

This might not seem very marketing-y, but if you don't meet the customer's expectations, no amount of extra-fancy marketing will make up for it.

Failing to deliver what you promised to deliver can't be covered up by a cute website, adorable packaging, or a popular blog.

If you've got the systems set up to fulfill your promises, then you can focus on **delight**. Like everything else, it depends on you and your people: *what would delight them?*

Fill in the following worksheet to find out.

WORKSHEET: DELIGHT YOUR PEOPLE

Rewrite the qualities of your business from page 34. (*Everything in your package should reflect these qualities.*)

What information does your product need to be useful to the user? (*Make sure this ends up on the label.*)

What do you want to say to your customer? (*Put this on a note and include it in the package!*)

Where can your customer connect with you? List options here. (*Include this on your note. You can print out cards that have this info and write your thank you note on them.*)

What was the last package you remember opening and loving? (*An iPhone, a book, a handmade something?*)

What made it so memorable?

Imagine that you are giving this item as a gift to your best friend and you could include anything—and cost was no concern. How would you wrap it or style it?

How can you scale this down to fit into the shipping container? (*Brainstorm lots of ideas here!*)

What do you want to try first?

Keep this worksheet handy so you know what to do with each order.

After a while, you'll get a little system for printing notecards, writing thank-you notes, and packaging everything up.

CUSTOMER SERVICE

The next aspect of **delight** is customer service. For most of our small businesses, this comes in the form of emails, so you want to have a system for reading and answering customer emails. This encompasses everything from the time it takes you to read an email, to knowing exactly what you want to say, and saying it in a way that's consistent with your brand.

To be prepared to handle everything, make some policies *before* you need them and clearly state them on your website (everything in your shop should link to your policies, or if you use Etsy or Artfire, make sure your policy page is up-to-date).

I know, policies don't *feel* like marketing, but they are. They give a potential customer confidence that you know what you're doing and that you're prepared to provide clear, easy-to-understand service. After the sale, you have something pre-stated to refer to when someone has a question.

That said, *stay flexible*. You want to answer every request with respect and understanding. The best thing you can do with a disappointed or angry customer is to let them know they're *heard*. Repeat back to them their concern and offer a solution, letting them know they have the option of accepting or rejecting that solution. A simple, *What can I do to make this right?* will go a long way to diffusing any situation.

For more than five years it's been my policy to replace absolutely anything that a customer isn't happy with (a replacement, not a refund). I let them keep the unsatisfactory item (and if it's something like the color was not what they expected, I encourage them to pass it along to a friend) and I ship a replacement (with a clear photo and their approval of the replacement piece). If they are really upset and say they don't want anything else, I offer a refund. (It's not an official policy, but at this point, I just want the customer to feel cared for and heard.)

So far, no one has taken advantage of it.

Take a risk and be generous with your policies. You can always change if your generosity is abused, but it's more likely that your generosity will be rewarded with repeat orders and customer referrals.

WORKSHEET: POLICIES

Payment
What methods of payment do you accept?

Shipping
When do you ship?

What do you use?

What does it cost the customer?

Do you contact them with the tracking number? When?

Returns or refunds
Under what circumstances do you offer a return or a refund?

What does the customer need to do? (How do they contact you? How soon do they need to say something?)

What will they get?

How soon?

Contact
How can everyone reach you?

Which do you prefer?

How soon should they expect a response?

THE VALUE OF REPEAT CUSTOMERS

Now we're here. At the place of happy customers. You've delighted, you've got clear policies, now you want to get that customer back (again and again). A repeat customer is far more valuable than a new customer. It costs less in marketing to get repeat customers to buy from you. They've already taken the leap once and you don't have to search them out—you already know who they are. You can spend less time on *convincing* and more time on *building* the relationship.

It's easy to focus all of our attention on finding new customers. Social media, craft shows, your website… most of it is aimed at finding and converting *new* people. There are a few big, easy ways to reach your past customers, so that's what we're going to focus on here. The first step is to get permission, then reach out to them on a regular basis.

You can put your customers in a special list on Twitter, or on Facebook, or ask them to subscribe to your blog… but the problem with social media is that your message might get lost in the busy stream of information. You want to make sure they see your reminder and that it comes right to them. In other words, you want to email them.

But be careful! You should not email any past customer without their consent. Buying from you is not a sign that they want to get emails from you every week (or month); you have to ask them specifically to sign up to receive your emails.

PERMISSION

Part of delighting your customers is communicating with them in a way they want. To stay in touch with your customers (and remind them to buy again), ask for their permission to contact them again.

I like to do this right when they purchase, by asking for their permission in my thank-you email— just a simple link to sign up for my newsletter, with a few words on what they can expect.

It looks something like this:

> *Thanks,* [name], *for your order!*
>
> *As a special thank you, I'm offering my customers a newsletter* [link to signup form] *that will include codes to secret sales, announcements, and free patterns for my yarns. Please sign up here* [link] *if you're interested.*
>
> *I'll mail your order this Wednesday with USPS Priority Mail. When I print the label, you'll get an email with a confirmation number, so you can track it as it travels to you! If you need it shipped sooner, just let me know.*
>
> *If you have any questions, comments, or would like a custom color or yarn, just hit reply!*
>
> *Tara*

If you don't have an email management account yet, now's a great time to set it up. Having a way to contact your customer on a regular basis is part of the strong foundation you're building, so we're going to go a little more into it right here.

REMINDING WITH EMAIL SOFTWARE

Even though we're talking about sending an email to your past customers, you can create email lists for anything: for the people you meet at craft shows, for the shops that sell your work, for the people who visit your website.

The first step is to set up an account with an email management software. I like Mail Chimp because it's easy to create emails and forms without needing to know anything technical. You *could* collect and manage email addresses on your own, without email management software, but I don't recommend it.

For starters, email management software is *very* affordable, even free for a small email list. On top of that, the software does all kinds of things you couldn't do easily. It:

- Generates a sign-up form. It can be a separate page or code for your sidebar.
- Keeps track of subscribes and unsubscribes.
- Puts an *unsubscribe* link at the bottom of every email, so you don't break any spam laws. (Yes—there are laws about this!).
- Helps you design a pretty email.
- Gives you stats on what got opened, clicked, and forwarded.

After you set up an account, figure out who you're sending email to. In this chapter, we're talking about emailing your past customers, so let's start there. You could also create a list (and a sign-up form) for people who visit your website and want to learn more, for the retail shops you work with, or for people you meet at craft shows (or all of the above could be on the same list).

Once you've decided *whom* you're emailing, think about *what* you want to send. As always, start with your outcome—why are you emailing? What's the outcome? What do you want the reader to *do*? If your objective is to have the subscriber remember how much they liked their purchase, you might want to send them a monthly email with your two or three best-selling items. If you want them to connect with you in a deeper way, you might send them an update of what's going on in your studio. If you want them to feel part of the larger community of buyers, then send them stories and pictures from your other customers—and while you're at it, ask them for their stories and pictures!

Some of the most popular emails:

- A free email series on something your user wants to learn about (*how to buy bridesmaid's jewelry*, or *how to pick a pattern to knit*, or *how to buy art you love*). These are scheduled as "autoresponders" which are automatically sent after a subscriber signs up.
- Weekly "what's new" emails, which have the inside scoop on what's new in your shop. (This is particularly effective and interesting if everything you sell is one-of-a-kind and they can't get

another one like it.) Another version could be "what's popular," where you share what's the best-selling thing in your shop. Make sure to include big pictures and an in-depth description, along with a link for the reader to buy the item directly from the email.

- Monthly traditional newsletters (these tend to be a round-up of what else is happening in your world: blog posts, new items, etc.). I don't like these much and my unscientific studies show that they aren't very effective for anyone's crafty biz.

What you send will help you decide when to send. Most marketing studies agree that sending often is more effective than *less* often, but what "often" means will be different for each audience. My yarn customers have responded well (in terms of both opening and buying) to weekly emails that listed the newest yarns (especially since each yarn was unique—if they missed it, they couldn't get it again). Any longer than five or six weeks and your subscribers will forget that they ever signed up and might even mark the message as "spam" without ever opening it. Experiment with what works for your business.

Now, proper care and management of your email list (and writing compelling, effective emails) could be a book unto itself. For now, just keep referencing what you know about your Right People. Write what interests them, while sharing your message. If you continue to do that, while learning from what they tell you (watch your open and click stats), you're off to a great start.

Here are a few more quick tips to get you started:

- If you want your reader to take an action (buy this item, click this link), make that the only thing you ask them to do in the email. Don't distract them with "follow me on Twitter," "comment on my blog," or "read this article." The more options you give, the less likely they are to do what you want (or to do anything at all).
- Make that one action clear and direct. Say "click here" or "buy it here."
- Include the entire, spelled-out link of what you want them to do, in case their email software stripped it (e.g., http://taraswiger.com).
- Don't start your email with an apology. Even if you haven't sent an email in six months, your readers probably don't remember. Don't remind them.
- Ask questions! End your email with an invitation to tell you something specific. (Bonus points: include the actual words "hit reply" and more people will do it.) Make your question have specific value for the customer: *Hit reply to tell me what color I should make next and I'll name it after you,* or *Got a favorite flower? Hit reply to tell me and I'll create a necklace inspired by it.* Remember: don't ask for feedback if you want them to click BUY. Save the questions for a separate email.

REFERRALS + TESTIMONIALS

Now that you've completely delighted and satisfied your customer, it's time to ask them to confess their love. Everyone knows about word-of-mouth marketing, but how do you get it? *You ask for it.*

In this section we're going to talk about the marketing power of your biggest fans—referrals and testimonials. Referrals are when a fan tells someone about you. A testimonial is when a fan gives you a quote to use in your materials. Both are powerful, but a referral is that slippery, hard-to-measure gold standard of marketing. It is that longed-for "word of mouth."

Before you read on, take a minute to think about how referrals could help you. If your thing is an investment of time or money, a referral will reassure a potential buyer that it's worth the investment. If your thing is personal and involves working and talking with you, a referral can reassure a potential buyer that you're nice and friendly, not scary. Here's another way to measure if you could benefit from spending your time on referrals: if you get a lot of looky-loos (views in your Etsy shop, people in your craft show booth), but not a lot of buyers—you need referrals. There's something stopping the person who likes your item from actually purchasing it. Either the investment required or something else about purchasing from you seems risky—double check that your policies are clear to help allay this fear! Hearing from a friend that your stuff is awesome, or reading a testimonial, might be just the thing to push them closer.

Referrals are what your customers tell their friends. It's a tweet: *Hey, I love the earrings I got from @designateddryden!* It's a comment in a conversation: *Oh, I love my hairstylist!* It's also when someone in your network (one of your peers) recommends you to their customer: *If you buy this pattern, you might want to make it with Velma's yarn.* This last kind of referral is what a lot of service providers (photographers, hairdressers, etc.) rely on, but product-makers can benefit from them too.

REFERRALS AND SOCIAL OBJECTS

Referrals are a sort of currency. In relationships, we exchange information: stories, confidences, and recommendations. Throughout a relationship, you're building trust. When you recommend something, you're imbuing it with the trust you've earned. This is why we're often hesitant to recommend something we're not thrilled with… it's *our* reputation on the line.

Hugh McLeod calls the thing we talk about a "social object." A social object can be anything; it's the thing our conversation is centered on. A social object is meaningful to a group of people; it's worth talking about.

An example in the knitting world is the Clapotis pattern from Kate Gilbert. Thousands of people have knit a Clapotis and you know it when you see it. When you're at a fiber festival, you might see several. But when you're walking through your small town and you see one? It's a sudden conversation starter. It's a public sign that you're part of a secret society of knitters. It's more than just a shawl, or a pattern; it has meaning for a group of people who like to talk about it.

When you're in the know, when you understand the object being discussed, you earn "social capital."

To a group of elementary school kids, social capital might be knowing all the lyrics to a pop song. To a high schooler, it might be having the right shoes. As an adult woman, having one-of-a-kind, handmade earrings (*Oh these? These were made by a math-nerd in Portland!*) might be social capital.

You want your thing to be a social object. You want it to be the currency that friends are exchanging. You want it to be the thing that people feel cool (or smart or fancy or punk) for knowing about. You want to know how social capital works, so you can communicate the desirability to your Right People. Because you're not just selling to them, you're also giving them a story to tell their friends; you're arming them with social capital.

Remember: people *love* giving referrals. Humans are built to share. Your job isn't to convince them to share your thing, but to make it irresistibly shareable.

SOMETHING IS IRRESISTIBLY SHAREABLE WHEN IT'S EASY TO SHARE AND IT'S SPECIAL.

Make it easy to share

Give your thing handles (metaphorical handles). Handles are what makes your thing easy to grasp and easy to convey. If your thing is online, that means a button for Twitter, Facebook, and whatever social media your people use. Send it in an email, so they can forward it to their friend.

Wherever your person purchases your thing, they should get all the information they need to be able to share its story with someone else. This can be the description on a website, a label, or a tag on the item. This is not just your core message, but the story of the particular item. What's interesting about it? What about it would someone want to share with a friend?

Make it special

If your items are one-of-a-kind (like a hand-spun skein of yarn, which can never be recreated exactly), this is built right in. Make sure you highlight it! If you make multiples of your products, create a series (or maybe just one piece a season) that is completely unique. That one-of-a-kind piece should be more outrageous and more expensive than all your other pieces. Even if you never sell it, people will talk about it.

Tiffany (the jeweler) became famous for buying a 128-carat yellow diamond. He never sold the diamond (Tiffany's still owns it), but it's definitely worth talking about and telling other people about. And once you go into the shop to see it… why not just go on and buy a piece of (smaller, less expensive) jewelry there?

And if you do sell that one, huge piece, you better believe that buyer is going to tell everyone she knows about it.

Get referrals

People are looking for something to share, and you are creating shareable things—so how do you get those people to share your shareable stuff? You make sure they know about it (via all the marketing you learn in this book) and you ask them to share. I don't suggest asking people to share a specific post or product out of the blue. Instead, focus on getting someone who already knows and loves your work to share it and to refer it.

HOW TO ASK FOR A REFERRAL

1. Make someone blissfully happy.
Obviously, the person who is referring you and your work needs to **love** your product. You'll create this experience by doing exactly what you've promised to do—and then a little more. Make sure your product arrives on time, presented in a way that reflects your brand, and with a personal note.

2. While they're in the midst of being happy, ask them to tell someone else.
While the person is fresh from opening your product, ask them to share it. You can set a reminder on your calendar, maybe one week after you've shipped the item (or made a sale in person) to email the person, asking them how they liked your product and asking them to share it.

3. Give them the tools they need to tell someone else. Make it easy to share by crafting a tweet or an email they could send to someone they think would like it. Or ask them to sign up for your newsletter (and make your newsletter shareable).

CREATE A SYSTEM

You've done everything you can to make your thing *really* referrable, and it's possible that people are starting to refer it all on their own. But kick it up a notch and create a system that asks for the referral (or testimonials). One week after you ship an item, plan to send an email (or set up an autoresponder in your email software) and ask the customer how they like the item.

When they reply, take a sentence or two of what they said (edit it if you need to, in a way that makes it clear, but doesn't change the meaning) and ask them if you can use this as a testimonial. Most people are delighted to have you share their words.

While you're asking for the testimonial (or if they don't say anything quotable), ask them to tell a friend. You can give them a code that earns them a discount for every friend they refer, or just ask them to tweet about their experience. As part of your normal week's marketing schedule, add their testimonial to your site. It can go on a special "praise" page, or on the bottom of your item descriptions, or you can collect testimonials throughout the month and share them all in an email. But don't let the testimonials sit there in your inbox—use them to decorate your business's home!

ALWAYS BE LISTENING

The last feature of an effective home is having a system for listening. In the next chapter we're going to talk more about listening to what your *potential* customers say, but for now, let's look at how you can listen to what your *existing* customers say.

You can get feedback from your customers by asking for it and by paying attention to what they're already telling you. The easiest way is to pay attention to what they tell you. If they send feedback in an email, put all these emails in a folder. If you hear the feedback in person or on the phone, whip out a notebook and write it down so you remember it for later. I like to collect everything in a folder in Evernote and review it every time I have a decision to make.

Now, you can wait around for these emails and comments to drip in or you can create a system for gathering them. Use the same system you have for gathering referrals and testimonials—ask your customer right after they purchase your product. Go on and put this on your calendar so you don't forget. Lots of people won't answer, but be sure to thank those that do and answer any questions they have! If the buyer suggests a change that will make the process easier, note it and schedule to do it right away. Don't let this feedback just sit idly in a folder waiting for "free time."

You can also get feedback by sending out surveys. You can ask for ideas on what your next product should include or feedback on what you've done so far. One tip: people don't know what they want or what they'd pay, so avoid questions like, "How much would you pay for X." Instead ask something like, "Have you used X in the past? What was the benefit?"

What should you collect from customers?
*   stories
*   pictures
*   examples of using your product
*   testimonials

In both natural feedback and surveys you want to pay attention to:
*   what your customers like about you and your product (do more of this!)
*   what words they use (make sure to use this language in your next description)
*   interesting stories or uses of your products that you hadn't considered

Now that you've got some stories and pictures, put them to use! You can use these on your blog, your shop, your social media accounts, in your craft show booth, or in the press. Just be sure to ask the individual if you can use their story. If you edit it at all (and you might want to!), be sure to send them an edited version and get their approval. Most fans will be delighted to be featured and appreciated, but honor those who aren't.

Some ideas:
*   Highlight your customers' stories on your blog (maybe a monthly Spotlight on Our Fans series).
*   Put their pictures in your sidebar.
*   Send out a customer's story of using your item to your email list.
*   Post a quote on your Facebook wall.
*   Use a great picture in your product listing (if you've got their permission).
*   Write a press release all about your customer, and send it to the local press, pitch it to the appropriate magazine, or write a blogger about it.

This will be much more effective if what you're sharing is truly a story, not just a gush of love for you and your product. How did the customer use your scarf during the Snow-pocalypse? What did the bride say when your customer gave her the specially monogrammed sheets?

If your customer sends you a glowing testimonial then use it as a testimonial, but feel free to reply and ask for a story. Something like, "I'm so glad you love it! How have you been using it? How have you been wearing it? I'd love to see pictures of it in its new environs!"

WELL, NOW, ISN'T THAT A LOVELY HOME!

If you've worked through this chapter, tweaked your site, delighted your customers, and started asking for referrals, then you've built more than a standard split-level. You've crafted a castle! Keeping a tidy and inviting home is a regular (if somewhat tedious) task. But the oohs and ahs you get as strangers are transformed into delightful party guests will be well worth the effort. Now take off that apron, Cinderella, and jump into a party gown, because we're about to go out on the (virtual) town.

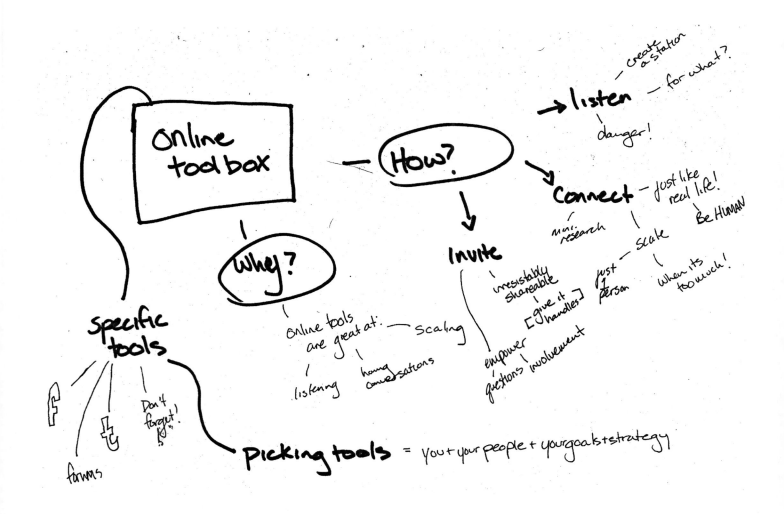

Online tool box

Why?

How?

→ **listen** — create a station — for what?

danger!

Connect — Just like real life!

mini research | just — scale | Be HUMAN

Invite

irresistably shareable

[give it handles]

just 1 person

when its too much!

empower questions involvement

Online tools are great at: — Scaling

listening   having conversations

specific tools

f

t g

Don't forget!

forums

Picking tools = you + your people + your goals + strategy

CHAPTER 5: ONLINE TOOLS

You're clear on what makes *you*—and what *you* make—unique. You've got a good definition of your Right People and you've created a great home base for them to visit…. Now you're ready to begin the *go-out-and-get-people* parts of marketing.

If you picked up this book thinking, *Ugh, I hate Twitter… I hope she doesn't tell me how great it is,* relax! I'm not going to try to make you love (or use) any particular tool. (If I did, this book would be out of date faster than I can type it.)

Remember: they're only tools. You are the toolbox owner and you get to decide *what* to use and *when* to use it. There's no tool so fabulous that you have to use it even if you hate it.

Using marketing tools is a lot like using your craft tools. You don't just buy the coolest new gadget… you think about what you want to make and what you want it to do. If you're a knitter, you probably don't pay attention to the newest kind of glitter. If you're a jewelry maker, you probably don't worry about the brands of scrapbooking paper.

And so it is for your marketing—you take what you learned about you and your message; you take into consideration where your people are going to be; and then you choose (or reject) tools based on that information.

By "tools," I mean anything you use online to connect, listen, and talk to your Right Person. This might be a blog, Twitter, Facebook, Google+, email, forums, or something that hasn't been created yet. Online tools are always changing but no matter *what* you use, you need to learn both how to use it technically (logging in, searching, etc.) and how to use it to build a relationship. Instead of going into detail about using one tool (or even the best tools), I'm going to cover relationship-building principles that you can apply to *any* tool.

> If your business is bricks and mortar, don't skip the online tools! And if your business is entirely online, don't skip the offline tools. No matter what you sell, you'll want to use a mix of both.
>
> We'll get more into how to build your strategy and your particular mix of tools in Chapter 7.

No matter what tool you use, it has to fit into your overall strategy and be something your Right People use. Once you're sure of this, you can use *anything* to listen, build trust, make your thing more findable for your Right People, and collect those referrals and testimonials that will seduce more people to trust you.

We're going to start with *why* you might want to use online tools and then assess whether they match up with your objectives and how to know if a tool is right for you and your people. Then we'll talk about how you want to be using online tools, what they're uniquely suited for, and how they can help you build relationships. At the end of the chapter, there's a list of tools that suit *everyone* and every kind of business (hint: you're probably already using them).

WHY USE ONLINE TOOLS?

Online tools, for all their differences, allow you to do things you can't do offline. They let you listen in on what your people are saying and what they want (in a non-creepy way!). You can also use online tools to connect to people that you'd never meet in your regular world—the weird, the wonderful, the delightfully just-like-you. And all that listening and connecting doesn't just benefit you, it benefits your people. Your people can use social tools to check out your reputation, talk to others about their experience with your products, and shout their love for your thing to the rooftops. This means you've got a stronger connection to a broader swath of people.

"Listening" may sound a little stalkery, but I promise it's not. In fact, this is the easiest, least market-y way to interact with social media. Instead of you telling people about your thing, you're just going to listen to them—what they like, what they don't like, and what they want. You're not going to tap people's phones, you're simply going to find what they're already publicly sharing—on Twitter, on Facebook, on their blogs, in forums. Anywhere where your people are talking about what you make (whether it's your brand or someone else's), you can pay attention. Listening takes very little time and maintenance, but can teach you so much about what to make and how to share it.

Building relationships anywhere is the same: you meet people; you share things; you build trust through continuing to share and reply and listen. What's different about using online tools to build relationships is that every step in the process is magnified and made easier. You have access to so many more people. And those people have joined together in little pockets based on similar interests. It is much easier to share things (especially links and media) than in person. (*Have you ever tried to tell someone about your favorite song? Using online tools, you can share the song, not just your love for it.*) And you can share the stuff you love (and experience the stuff they love, and their opinions) more consistently (every minute, if you want). Your interactions are now time-shifted—you don't have to be physically present (or even awake) for a new friend to share something with you—and they don't have to be present when you reply to it.

Now that you're building relationships with potential customers, you want to remember this: building relationships is the same, it's only that ease of use has changed. Even though you CAN send a link 50 times in a week, would you do that in real life? (*Would you call up that potential buyer 50 times in a week to tell them about one item?*) I hope not!

Online tools allow your people to find each other and talk about your thing. This is terrifying for a company with lousy products and poor customer service, but for an artist like you, this can be *wonderful.* People can share your product (and how they use it) through photos, links, videos, and referrals. They can share it with their own social group and with the community of other buyers. Online tools allow you to introduce these people to each other (or allow them to find each other) so they can share their enthusiasm. And when your customers talk about you on social media, those conversations are public to the rest of their (*not-yet-your-customer*) social circle.

Now that you know what online tools are particularly well-suited for (listening, connecting with a vast group and creating social presence), it's time to actually try it.

HOW TO LISTEN

Sounds a bit icky, right? But you won't be tapping phones; you'll just start listening to what people are already sharing publicly. To start, you'll create a **listening station‡**—a place where you can collect what's being said about you, your product, and your industry. Then you'll listen to your community by asking them questions and engaging in their conversations. Finally, you'll **do something** with what you learn from listening.

Your listening station is the place where you collect everything you want to listen to. This is really just a collection of searches that you've saved, on everything from your name to your product category. The easiest way to listen is to start with a tool that will collect several searches and report back what it finds on a regular basis: Google Alerts. Go to alerts.google.com and set up your first search, following their directions. You should do separate searches for your name (first and last together, in quotation marks, like "Tara Swiger"), your business name (again, in quotation marks), any specific names of your products (e.g., "month of love yarn" or "veritas shawl" or "flight earrings"), and finally, all possible misspellings (e.g., "blond chicken," "blondechicken," "tarah swieger"). Yes, this is a lot, but many of the misspellings will never turn up any results (and thus, you won't get an alert for it).

This is a fine place to stop for a beginner, but if you're also on Twitter, set up a search there. Start with misspellings of your Twitter handle (without the @), and add on your name and your business name. Make sure each of these is separate search, or you'll only get results that include all the words in one tweet (unlikely!). After each search, click "save this search" and this search will appear in your saved searches. Different tools (Hootsuite, Tweetdeck) have options for you to save searches as streams, so click around on the tools you use and find out where your searches are hiding.

Above all, be sure to check these regularly! Old tweets don't stick around long, so check the most common ones (you'll learn which this is after a few weeks) once a week or so. Better yet, subscribe to the searches using a feed reader like Google Reader. That way the results will stay in your Reader until you see them.

A lot of your first searches will be for you, your brand, and your products. But as you become more comfortable listening, you'll want to start widening your searches to include other sources. Start listening to the people you're already talking to. This isn't just online, of course; you're going to start paying attention to what everyone is saying: your friends, strangers (especially when they're shopping

---

‡ *Chris Brogan coined the term 'listening station' and shares very detailed directions for creating one in his book* Trust Agents.

for what you make), the news, the world.

What does this have to do with marketing?
What you hear, read, and absorb is going to to affect how you deliver your message: both the content and voice of the message itself and what you use to deliver it.

WHAT ARE YOU LISTENING FOR?

Everything. More specifically, everything that has to do with *what* you do: from people's feelings about the product category (*I can only wear nickel-free silver earring-backs*), to Pantone's color reports and *In Style*'s report on the season's trends, to the specific feedback you get from the customer (*I love to wear it with a v-neck shirt*).

Here are some specific things to listen in on (this is by no means an exhaustive list):

- questions about use (*How do I wear it?*)
- questions about utility (*Why do I need that?*)
- comments about choice (*I wish it came in green.*)
- exclamations of joy (*What specifically do I like?*)
- trend reports on color, fashion, technology use, demographics
- news about the larger industry (*gifts*), the specific category (*stationery*), and your niche (*stationery for new moms*)
- comments from browsing shoppers, especially when they recommend something for each other (*Moms and daughters in a changing room are an endless source of comedy... and of marketing research, as are friends plotting a baby shower, or couples planning a dinner party.*)

WORKSHEET: WHAT TO LISTEN FOR

What search terms do you want to keep an eye on? (Include your name, your business name, your product names, and your product categories.)

Where will you search?
- ☐ Google alerts
- ☐ Saved Twitter search
- ☐ Other

What other information would you like to hear from your potential customers?

What information would help you in designing your next product?

Where might you "hear" this information?

What blogs talk about it?

What search terms might turn up results?

What magazines write about it?

Where do your customers naturally have these conversations?

Absolutely *everything* has the potential to be useful… *if* you have a way to capture it, process it, and turn it into action. To keep from getting buried in information, let's create a plan for how you're going to capture, think about, and process everything you hear.

Your capturing and processing style will depend on what works for you—so experiment! I like to use Evernote, an online and smartphone application, to save things I read, make notes about what I hear, and take pictures (or videos, or audio clips) of things I find interesting. I also keep a notebook in my purse at all times to write down snippets of ideas.

But I like (nay, *love*) words and I know they're the best thing to jog my memory. If you're more visual, try a mood board. You can create one using a bulletin board (or a journal, or a canvas) and images you cut out, create, or snap. Or you can create one online, using Pinterest, which allows you to grab photos from anywhere on the web. If you prefer to take photos of everything inspiring, you might just organize them on Flickr—or, heck, in the folders on your computer!

Whatever you use, you'll want to be able to find things easily so you can go back and re-experience the original inspiration. Instead of relying on my own ability to properly sort when I capture something, I prefer to use tags (although Evernote has a great search function that can search for a word anywhere—even in a PDF or image). When storing, ask yourself when and how you're going to want to see this again and use that to guide your sorting, tagging, or searching.

Now you have a collection of things. You're listening, you're gathering, you're storing—but how to process it?

EXPERIMENT WITH LISTENING

1. Listen and gather, making sure to grab at least one snippet (a conversation, a color you like, etc.), every day for a week.
2. At the end of the week, sit down with what you've gathered and a piece of paper.
3. Read through it all and then answer these questions:
   - What new product could you create inspired by what you read?
   - What one sentence do you want to include in your descriptions?
   - What question do your people have that you could answer in a blog post?
   - Sketch (with words or images) the person you captured that MOST wants what you're selling.

Variations on this experiment:
- Listen in with your current project in mind. Collect anything that inspires that project (could be a sales page, or a new collection, or a new blog post).
- Instead of reading through at the end of the week, do it every day for three minutes. Or every month for an hour.
- Instead of reading through it all at once, read one piece and let it inspire something. Then move on to the next.
- Make up your own questions.
- Instead of questions, start free-writing (or mind-mapping, or drawing).
- Write about what you'll change.
- Write about what you've done right.
- Write about what everyone else is wrong about.
- Write about how your thing will rock that one person's world.

This, again, depends on how *you* best work.

Some will want to schedule weekly (or monthly) times where they revisit what they captured. Others (like me) will prefer to glance through it when it's time do something (like writing a new sales page or creating a new product). This can also impact the way your inspiration affects your work: is it sparking new ideas? Are you using it to brainstorm? Or do you bring it in to help you figure out what's not working?

Try all of it. Try changing it up.

Experiment!

DANGEROUS EXPERIMENTS?

Implicit in all the listening exercises on the opposite page is a bit of danger. It can be easy to be swayed by what you read and hear. Perhaps you'll be inspired so strongly by something else that you'll make something just like it (or maybe you'll become so afraid of doing this that you choose to shut out the world). Perhaps you'll read and hear so much (especially about the economy, or people complaining about the cost), that the entire enterprise will seem hopeless. Perhaps you'll waste too many hours listening and not spend enough hours doing.

These are real dangers, and I have a few preventative measures to try. But above all, keep in mind the goal of *listening*: You want what you're learning to *inform* your work (making sure you answer the questions people are asking) without it changing the spark of *you* that is in your making, your writing, and your marketing.

PREVENTATIVE MEASURES

How to prevent copying: Don't look at, follow, or read people in your exact category.

Instead, be inspired by fields far different than yours. As a yarn-maker, I'm inspired by knit design, paintings, movies, gardens, and baking. Shannon's a jeweler who's inspired by math and engineering. Amy's an artist inspired by fiction, fantasy, games, and the community of die-hard fans.

If you're in fashion, instead of looking at fashion magazines, get your trend report from the color experts: Pantone. Get your fashion news from the streets, film, other cultures, and individuals you admire.

How to prevent wasting time: Set a timer.

Really, that's it. I like Focus Booster (http://focusboosterapp.com), because it allows me to work in 25-minute chunks, then take a five-minute break automatically. (That's how I wrote this chapter!) It only works if you actually close the tabs and walk away from the computer (or magazine) when the timer goes off.

How to prevent hopelessness: Shut out the Nervous Nellies and Debbie Downers.

Turn up the volume on your own happy, sparkly music (I created a Happy Sparkly station on Pandora.com for just such occasions, you can get the link at taraswiger.com/market-yourself.)

Whether you're bummed by ultra-successful crafty businesses or depressed by the failure of the ones you love, remember: only YOU can prevent forest fires (or economic apocalypse). Do what you need to do to make yourself fireproof (whatever that means for you: a "day job," a savings account, cutting out extra spending) and realize that nothing anyone else does (short of the IRS) is a reflection on your own capacity for growth and success.

THIS IS SLOW-GOING

Whew, we've talked a lot about online tools, and so far, I'm only telling you to *listen*. How in the world will anyone know what you have to say? Well, remember that the first step is to get clear on your message, then make sure it's clear on your website. That's because, in the beginning of a relationship at least, you're going to just talk to people about their stuff. One hopes that they will then click on your profile and click through to your site. If your site is clear, they'll see that you sell stuff, and see how they can find out more.

This is a passive method, but it's essential that you start **here**, first just connecting and getting comfortable with the online tool you're using. After a while, you're going to start *sharing* your message more proactively, but it's vital that you first have some conversations. For a new business, these conversations are the first feedback and contact you're having with your Possibly Right People. You'll start to see where and who your people are and what they say. For an established business, you will still want to take the time to build relationships and have conversations, to feel out a new tool and see what the culture is like. This will help you measure the appropriate doses of your marketing message and how to best share them with this audience.

The relationships you build will be with your core group of supporters and sharers. They'll give you feedback, help you name your new products, and spread the word (when you create something shareable). If you jump in with your marketing messages right away, the people you *might* connect with will think of you only as a marketer. There's another thing at play here: **social proof**. Having conversations and developing relationships with some people serves as proof to *other* people that you're worth talking to and paying attention to. When you first join a social media site, you start with zero friends. When new people see your profile, they don't know if you're a scammy marketer, or a delightful *you*. Building relationships (not just racking up friends, likes, and followers) will provide social proof that you're a real person and that other people have found you delightful, useful, and entertaining.

And that brings us to the next thing that the online world is particularly well-suited for: gathering social proof and connecting your people.

HOW TO CONNECT

The second thing that online tools are particularly well-suited for (besides listening) is connecting. And if you think about it, this is probably how you use these tools already. Email, blogging, comments, Flickr, forums—other than reading the news or looking up information, I bet that *everything* you do online right now is related to connection. It might not be focused on marketing, but you are *already* an expert at connecting online.

But there's something weird that happens to perfectly smart, generous crafters when they start to think about marketing online. Instead of connecting to customers in the way they've been connecting with friends, they begin to get stilted, odd, unhuman. Their tweets read like billboards and their blog becomes a commercial. Their emails become corporate-ish and they use phrases like "in regards to" or "I'm excited to tell you about."

Why?

It's because we think of *marketing* tools as different than *connecting* tools. Our cultural understanding of what *marketing* is (*broadcast sales messaging*) infects a normal conversation. We try to talk fancy, so people take our business seriously. We think that there must be some trick to marketing, something that's different from usual human interaction. *That's part of the reason you picked up this book, right?*

And you're right—to a point. Marketing is different than an email to your mom, because it has a goal. The goal is to share a message, your message. And that, the act of trying to share a message with people (instead of just saying whatever pops into your head), can feel weird. Maybe a little not-like-yourself. To help you get over this, we're going to look at what makes the connecting you're already doing work. We're going to dissect what's already working in the way you use online tools and then apply it to your business, using the filter of your message and your Right People.

What are you doing to connect with the people you're already friends with? You listen to them, reply, and share experiences. You ask them about themselves and then you really listen to what they say. When you see something you think they'd like, you share it with them. And finally, you share experiences together—whether it was surviving high school orchestra, or watching *Friends* every Thursday night, or laughing through a movie.

You can take each of those aspects and apply them online. You "follow" a person on Twitter or read their blog, then comment on what they've shared. You might check out their pictures on Flickr and tell them how cute their kid is. When they share something, you reply. (*Not to every single utterance*, of course. That's nearly impossible. Also, you'll look like a stalker.)

Once you know the person a bit better, you'll start to see stuff you know they'd like. You can deepen your connection by sharing those things with them. You can email them, tweet them, leave a post on their Facebook wall. I've sent friends books in the mail, emailed about a tool I thought she'd like, and even named yarns after the person it reminded me of.

Sharing experiences might seem a little harder to do online. There are two ways to do it— you can talk about a physical experience that you've both experienced (like when everyone is watching the same TV show at the same time and tweeting about it) or you can share a digital experience (being a part of a class and talking on the forums). Once you know someone, it's natural to do all of the above. It's a part of building relationships that comes naturally.

FRIENDS WITH BENEFITS

Remember in the chapter on Right People where we said that your Right People are your friends and encouragers AND your customers. Well, the temptation with connecting online is that you'll want to spend time with your friends and encouragers (because you know them, it's comfortable)… but the actual marketing benefit will come when you spend time connecting with future customers, with those Right People who actually want to buy what you sell. Of course you're still going to spend time online connecting with your friends and support group, but just remember that it *doesn't* count as marketing.

But where it gets harder (and where you might get weird) is when you scale this up from one-to-one to *one-to-many*. It's easy to connect to one person; we can easily remember what one person likes, we can invite one person to see a movie. But what about the group of people, your Right People? At any given time, you don't know exactly who is in that group, and (*ideally*) new people are always joining the your Right People Club.

So how do you scale up the skills you already have connecting with one person at a time to connecting to a group of people?

For starters, you **do connect** with some people one-on-one. When you first start your business and you don't have a pile of Right People lined up, the easiest way to figure out who your Right People are and what they like is to connect with individuals. You want to first do the worksheets from the Right People chapter, to be sure you're focusing in the right places (e.g., *you're connecting with other knitters when you really need to be connecting with buyers-of-baby-blankets*).

You connect with these individuals by finding them (check out page 47 for a reminder), listening to them, and then responding. At the same time, you'll be posting things (on your blog, Twitter, Facebook page) that you think they'll like. You don't have to say, "I think you'll like this…," you just *know* that they will. This is where all the listening you've done comes into play. You see the kinds of things they read and like, so you share that kind of information with them.

This can feel theoretical, so let's look at specific examples.

I make handspun yarn. People who buy it want to knit or crochet with it, so I share links to patterns (in books, magazines, online—not just mine!) that my people can make with handspun yarn. When someone (a past customer, a knitter I just met, etc.) posts a picture of something they made, I comment on it (especially if it's made out of handspun yarn, *anyone's* handspun yarn). When I first started on Twitter, I did a LOT of replying to other people's tweets. Not just "good job!" or "so funny!" but actual conversational tweets like "That's such a cool project! Have you ever been to Legoland?" or "Amazing color combo! It reminds me of apples + pumpkins." This is true on any tool you're using—respond for real.

Amy makes art and cards inspired by sci-fi and fantasy books (among other things). She's very active in the fan community (commenting on forums, emailing with other fans) but in her posts very rarely mentioned her shop (it's considered spamming in that community). Even though she rarely talks about her own thing, people have learned what she does (just as you learn what the dude you meet at the coffeeshop does, without him handing you a business card when he says hello) and this has led to many opportunities. Some of the friends she's made have bought something from her shop, others have commissioned large pieces, and still others have told their friends.

HAVING A CONVERSATION

When you're first getting started, you can move your business forward just by meeting and talking to people in the online community that you're trying to reach. This will give you practice in finding your Right People and jumping into conversations with them. It will instruct you on what they're looking for and the language they use.

In the beginning, you're going to be doing a lot of work just to *find* people and talk to them. Do not be discouraged if you don't get replies, comments, or see an immediate response to what you're putting out there. That's normal and to be expected. Getting started with a new tool can be a little like showing up at a party where you don't know anyone... and no one knows you.

But unlike a party at a stranger's house, newcomers are *welcomed* into online circles everyday. Part of the joy (for me) of social media sites like Twitter is that I meet new people every day. If you introduce yourself to others in a friendly, open manner and if you develop an online presence full of useful and interesting things, you'll start to get a bit of response.

In the beginning, response will come by way of replies (to your tweets, on your Facebook page, in your blog comments). Even though these are not yet customers, these responses are still valuable. A reply has a kind of value, because it signifies that someone isn't just silently consuming what you're sharing, but she's willing to take an action, she's willing to invest a few seconds in replying to it.

When she replies, your Right Person is taking a step *towards* you. She's reaching out. This is a necessary first step and learning how to get replies will also teach you how to get the response you want later in the relationship (*when the action you want her to take is to click "buy"*).

Before we get into replies and comments, a word of warning: the art of getting replies (and then replying, and having conversations) is an **addictive** one. We humans are social creatures and we crave feedback, and social media allows us to gather up more and more every day. It can be tempting to spend all our "marketing" time and effort just on collecting replies and conversation partners. But as part of a healthy marketing diet, remember that connecting and conversations are an indispensable part of your marketing plan—but only a part.

Now that you've been warned, let's talk about how to get the first few replies. In order to start conversations, we're going to take a two-pronged approach:

1. Ask for a response.
2. Reply to their reply.

Sounds simple, right?
It is!

On a regular basis, on whatever tool you're using, simply ask a question.

A few tips for asking good questions:
*   Make the question fun and easy to answer.
*   Make it about THEM (instead of about YOU or your business).
*   Leave it open-ended (you'll be surprised by the answers).
*   Ask your followers to vote on something fun. (Whenever I redo my hair color, I let Twitter vote: pink or blue?)

Once you do get a reply (to a tweet, a blog post, etc.), the next step is important: **reply back**. But before you do, try this trick I learned from Mari Smith's book *The New Relationship Marketing*—click through, learn a bit about them, and *then* reply. The extra step of mini-research doesn't need to take more than a few minutes, but can make all the difference in deepening a relationship or turning a stranger into a friend.

Let's look at a few examples.

You post a link to something your Right Person would love (a new online magazine). Ann replies "Thanks for that link!" You can simply reply "You're welcome." and that will be the end of that conversation.

Examples of tweets with mini-research that open a conversation

Instead, click through to Ann's profile. Read her profile and her last few tweets. You see that she posts daily photos of her outfit and loves fashion. Now you can respond with, "You're welcome! P.S. Love those shoes you have on!" or "You're welcome! Did you see the cute bracelet on page 14?" (Ideally, you'll mention something that she'll probably like).

Ann may reply or she might not, but now you've got at least an opening for a conversation.

Yes, this mini-research takes time. It takes thought. But that's what makes this a *marketing* exercise, and not just *recreational* use of online tools. By doing mini-research, you're both learning more about your Right People and you're connecting with them. You're building a relationship that may turn this person into a buyer or into someone who recommends their friends to you.

TALKING TO MORE THAN ONE PERSON

Talking one-to-one is just the beginning. As your business grows and you reach more people, you'll want to be able to connect one-to-many, and you'll want to scale beyond a single conversation into many conversations. But how do you do that? How do you take skills meant for one person and branch them out to reach many?

For starters, you do the same thing, you just make it more public. Instead of replying to one person's question in an email, you post the reply (because it's likely more people have that question) in a blog post. Instead of having an IM conversation, you have a conversation on Twitter or Google+ or Facebook. Instead of asking one person a question, you ask on social media, and you open it up to everyone. Instead of posting a link to a crafty tutorial on your friend's Facebook wall, share it with the world via your business's page (or any other public sharing tool).

This is another place where things can get weird. When you were talking to one person, you probably sounded like yourself. But when you begin to write to many people, to write a blog post instead of an email, you might get more general and vague. Or worse still, you might start using more "professional" language and bigger words. In other words, you stop sounding like a person and start sounding like a faceless "business." *Blah.* This is no good.

The trick to continuing to sound like yourself when you're connecting to many people, when you're sharing widely, is to picture *just* one person. Imagine your Most Right Person. Maybe you know her already; maybe you don't. Just bring her, fully formed, into your mind when you write anything. Share links she'd like. Write blog posts answering her question. Tell her why and how you do what you do (and how it benefits her).

When you're just too popular

You're replying to all your replies, you're doing mini-research… and suddenly you're doing nothing else. There comes a point where you just can't do that anymore; the volume of replies is greater than you could keep up with (and still do your other work). Let's talk about how you know you're there, what to do about it, and how to keep your people happy as you scale up. When you inevitably become a household brand and überpopular designer, you'll want to have a plan in place for continuing to use social media to market your business, without drowning in it. Without a plan, it may feel like your only option is to reply to everything (and get nothing else done) or go completely offline. Although that sounds extreme, I've worked with several entrepreneurs who got to that point—where they were afraid to post anything to social media, for fear of angering the people they "owed" replies to.

So let's first get clear about one thing: you don't "owe" a reply to anyone who isn't a paying customer. We're replying to people (and researching them a bit first) in order to build relationships and make connections with your future Right People. If something comes up, and you can't reply *it will be alright.* No one will hate you, and you can keep posting new information and talking to people.

How to know when it's time to scale back
This is going to be different for everyone, but the first clue is that you're feeling overwhelmed at the thought of keeping up with replies.

First, some ground rules: we're **not** talking about keeping up with everyone else's tweets, Facebook updates or blog posts. We're talking about replying to the people who have replied to you, who have commented or asked a question to *you.* Also, we're not talking about the personal stuff. If you use any social media tools for both your business stuff and your personal stuff, we're only concerned with the business-y contacts. If your mom tweets you about picking up some milk for her, that doesn't count as a business obligation. *And fulfilling your personal obligations while running a succesful indiebiz is a subject for a whole other book!*

Before you cut back on replies (*or before you start slacking in your other work in order to keep up with social media*), do yourself a favor and start tracking your time. I like LetsFreckle.com for a quick (and free) timer. I find it helps me single-task (and get more done) and gives me a good idea of what I'm spending time on. Once you've tracked your time, you can more clearly see what you're spending time doing, and if keeping up with social media is a big chunk of that.

IS IT TIME TO SCALE UP?
TIME TO LET YOURSELF OFF THE HOOK FOR EVERY REPLY?

1. Do you get a sense of dread or feel overwhelmed right before logging into the social network?
2. Does replying feel like a chore and not like a fun conversation?
3. Are you skipping some replies because you either can't see them in the shuffle or you just don't have time?
4. Are you spending more time replying than creating new stuff (content, products, anything you might create for your business).

If the answer to any of these is yes, then it's time to think about how you can scale your replies and still interact with your community. This is where your timer comes in handy. Instead of trying to answer everything, or even the prioritized messages, set a timer and commit to answering for only X minutes. (The time will depend on you. I like ten-minute chunks, a few times a day.)

To figure out what needs your reply, consider your strategy (more on this in Chapter 7): Why are you using this tool to begin with? What are you trying to communicate? And who are you trying to communicate with?

- Your first priority is to your paying customers, *always*. If they have a question, reply to it.
- Your next priority is to someone who wants to be a paying customer. These people might ask questions like, "How soon can you ship this?" and "Is it available in blue?" You don't want to miss out on replying to them, and your response time might be the difference between getting the sale or not.
- After that is *everything else*. You can prioritize this further by looking at things that are on-topic for your message vs. off-topic, or you can just go in order (I like to reply to the oldest first, and move forward… but I only go back about one day).

And the replies you can totally skip? Ones that are impersonal and don't indicate they want a reply. These are ones like "good job!" or "love it!" or "ugh, that's awful!"

To make sure you remember your priorities when you jump online, fill out the worksheet on the next page.

WORKSHEET: REPLYING TO REPLIES—THE MASTER PLAN
(AKA *a contract with yourself*)

My first priority are past and current customers. They might ask questions like:

My second priority are potential customers. They might ask questions like:

Finally, everyone else—I'm going to approach them (circle one) oldest first or newest first. When necessary, I'll explain my commnication policy to people (maybe even post it on my website). That policy is:

I hereby promise to not feel guilty when I can't keep up. Instead of feeling like I've failed, I'll remember that this deluge of communication is a sign that I've succeeded in building a community around the work I love.

_____

Signature of Amazing Business Owner
Woo!

HOW TO INVITE YOUR PEOPLE IN

Online tools don't just put the power in *your* hands, they also empower your people. Just as you use online tools to connect with new people and share good stuff you find, your fans do too. They're also on the lookout for the best stuff (information, products, tips) to share with their circle of friends and fans. If you create the kind of stuff they want to share, you (and your stuff) will be what they share.

By empowering your people, you're making it easier for them to share your stuff with other people who will like it. Having others sharing your site, your shop, or your blog post makes your job (spreading your message) so much easier. It amplifies your message in a way you could never do on your own. Not only are more people hearing about your thing, it's also more of the Right People. (If your Right Person is doing the sharing, she's got influence with people who like and trust her, people that are more like her than not, therefore—more Right People.)

You can also empower your people by inviting them to be a part of what you do. This can include taking surveys, asking a question after the sale, letting them name a product or line, featuring them on your blog, or any number of things. Their involvement in your business connects them to your goal and mission. It gives them a reason to share it. (*Check out this yarn that I helped name!*) It doesn't just serve as another means of marketing; it will also help you build a better, more responsive business. You'll get insight into what your customers want and how they speak. You'll have first-hand research for the next time you create a product or introduce a new color.

How do you empower your people to share your message? You start with your content (both the *general*: your brand, shop, site; and the *specific*: a blog post, a tweet, physical products), then make it irresistibly shareable (more on this in a moment). When your content is irresistibly shareable, your people will want to share what you create and it'll be easy for them to do it. Once you have irresistibly shareable content, you ask them to share it. You watch and listen to what they say and how they say it and make notes. As you learn from what they share (and what they don't), you continue to tweak, create more irresistible content, and build on what you've learned. As an advanced step, you can even create events and reasons for your people to connect to each other and build a community.

The first step to getting people to share what you create is to **make it share-able**. You can do this simply by adding "sharing" buttons to your site, your shop, and anything else you want them to share. This can be a "tweet this" or "like it on Facebook" button or any other social media tool your Right People use. Take note—this is not the same as "follow me" or "friend me" buttons. The latter allow other people to follow what you share (which is a good thing), while the former allow the person to share your content to their own followers and friends.

IRRESISTIBLY SHAREABLE

Of course, adding "share this" buttons is just the bare minimum. It only makes your content able to be shared; it doesn't make people *want* to share it. You still have to make your content so good that people want to share it. You have to make it Irresistibly Shareable.

HOW ONE CRAFTER MAKES HER THING MORE SHAREABLE

Now, when Amy shares a piece of art, she doesn't just list it in her shop and leave it there. She writes a blog post about the piece of art. She shares some extra pictures, she talks about her inspiration and process. She mentions both the technical aspects (what paper, what paint, what process), but also the usability aspects (where it might look good in your house, how to frame it). These posts are much more shareable than just the item itself, because stories are shareable. Inspiration is shareable. Insight into someone else's process (even if they're a painter and you're a biologist) is shareable.

On the practical side of things, Amy includes a simple sentence in her post footer: "*Think a friend would like this? Share it with them,*" followed by a few "share me" buttons. Once she's written the post, she shares it on Twitter and her Facebook page, with a friendly tweet (Not: *New blog post: [link]*, but: *From the heart of a monster: Frankenstein's Love [link]*). Her post is shareable, her tweet or Facebook status is shareable, the entire thing is extra-shareable.

How can she make it even more shareable? Let's just brainstorm a list of things, no matter how crazy, and then Amy can take what will work best for her people and her business:

- Create a weekly (or biweekly) email of the week's best work. People who sign up will be getting a curated collection of Amy's prodigious work without having to keep up with her blog.
- Create a "buy a friend art" page that explains how to buy art for a friend.
- Create a "Want some art? Forward this to a friend" page that explains how to ask for art as a gift (and has tweet-able and email-able templates for the customer to copy and paste).
- Create a series on something in the news or potentially shocking.
- Create a series (of art or blog posts) inspired by people you know online and send them the link to the thing they inspired.

Amy has done just about everything to make her art shareable—have you?

WHAT DO YOU WANT SHARED?

There are many things you want people to share—the general (your shop, your site, your product line) and the specific (a product, a blog post). This requires an approach that includes opportunities for people to share both the general and specific. Your website, each item, and each blog post will all have "share" buttons. You'll make both your individual blog posts and your whole shop in the social media places you use easily shareable. You'll make it simple for your fans to share an individual item and the general shop. To do this, you'll go through the process of creating something Irresistibly Shareable twice—once for the general and once for the specific (well, in actuality, you'll make every new, specific thing irresistibly shareable).

ASKING FOR THE SHARE

Up until now, you've done everything you can to make your work share-able, which is the vital first step. If you don't have something that people are excited to share, it doesn't matter how much you ask them to share it. They won't. (Or if they do, it won't make an impression on the people they share it with.)

Now that you've made your work shareable, you're ready for the next step—the actual sharing. Once you've got your various online profiles set up, sharing is as simple as linking to something. But what do you do before you have any kind of online presence? How do you share your brand new shop or website? How do you enter the online world? Well, you'll start with the beginning of this chapter. You'll create accounts with the tools you want to use, then you'll listen in and start to connect.

That's the only answer.

You simply can't start sharing your products until you have people to share them with (picture an only child trying to learn how to share toys while he's all alone in his crib). And if you start your online relationships by talking about your own thing, you won't build much of a relationship. Once you have relationships, you want to maintain them, while sharing your work.

Many sweet, artistic types worry that if they start sharing, they'll automatically push people away, that every act of linking to their own thing somehow harms their relationships. Please, remember: it doesn't have to. Remember social capital? Sharing a link or information or something you think someone will like isn't a selfish act, it's a helpful one. Just because you made the thing you're sharing doesn't change the equation. If you're creating the thing your Right People want and will love, you're doing them a favor when you tell them about it. You are strengthening your relationship because you're sharing something personal, something meaningful to you.

That is, *if you do it in that spirit*. If you share the story behind the product, if you tell a story, if you provide a solution, and if you share it with a helpful, not-pushy intention, it can build a relationship. I know, this might sound hard to believe, especially if you've had experience with those crafters whose Twitter stream is an unending wave of links to their newest products. But instead of those spammers (and that's what they are) you are going to weave your products and blog posts into the fabric of your online relationships.

For example, Kristine designs knitting patterns. If you see her wearing one of her own designs and you compliment her and she doesn't give you the pattern information, you'd be bummed (if you're a knitter). You complimented it and you *want to know more*. You want to know where you can get one (or at the very least, you're curious). When Kristine says, "Thanks, it's my own design!" she isn't spamming you—she's sharing information you wanted. When you express interest and she hands you a card with the link, you're delighted. You've just connected. You now know more about her and her work and you probably feel a little closer to her than you did before you talked. This is exactly what you're doing online.

Now that you've got a handle on how online tools can be used to find and connect to your Right People, let's look at actually using and choosing those tools.

HOW TO KNOW WHAT TOOL IS RIGHT FOR YOU

The first question people want to know about online tools is: What should I be using? As always, you're the only one who can answer this. It depends on your people, and your message, and you. Let's start with you first (because even if your people use a tool, but you hate it, you won't use it).

Keep in mind when you're choosing a tool that *you* get to determine how you use it. *You* get to decide how public or private you want to be. *You* get to decide how much time it takes in your day. And above all, you have permission to not use it—even if it's the most popular thing since ice cream.

Of course, you can't really understand the appeal of most tools until you start using them. This is especially true of social media, where the fun is in the *social* aspect. Until you get social on it, you won't see what the fuss is all about. It's easy to decide against a tool before you really get to know it (*I don't have time for that! Ugh, a learning curve!*), but at the very least, run a new tool through the following process.

WORKSHEET: CHOOSING AN ONLINE TOOL

1. Start by looking at what people claim the tool does. (Read a bit about it, where people share their first person experience.) What does this tool offer to do that others don't?

2. Know yourself. What do you like to do online? How do you like to connect to people?

3. What are you comfortable with (photography, writing, sharing links, sharing your location)? How does this tool help you do that? Does this tool rely on you doing things you're not comfortable with (writing, sharing links, sharing locations)?

4. Your objectives: what do you want to get out of this tool? And overall, what do you want to have more of in your business?

5. Does this tool provide that?

6. Is this the kind of tool your people like to use? Is it something they'd use to find what you sell?

Now, there's no reason not to use online tools just for fun (I have yet to find a good business reason to play Bejeweled… but I don't plan on stopping any time soon), but if you think you're using it for marketing and it doesn't meet your marketing needs, rethink either that tool or your tactics for using it. (We'll get into your marketing objectives in Chapter 7.)

Remember: you have permission to use only what works for you!

That brings us to another question: how do you know what works for you? Experiment.

HOW TO CREATE AN EXPERIMENT

Create a small, doable experiment, measure the results and decide what works.

Steps to creating an experiment:
1. Set your goals in quantifiable, measurable metrics. (Example of a good metric: get two new people a week on my newsletter. Example of a weak metric: get more readers.)
2. Look at your goals, look at the tool, and create a plan that will help you reach those goals. Don't just jump right in; really look at what you can do with that tool to create the results you want.
3. Set a timeline. How long will this experiment last?
4. Put the plan in motion.
5. At the end of the time, look at your metric. Did it change how you wanted it to? Look at other metrics too—if you were trying to get more blog readers, but your newsletter subscriptions went up, that's notable! Or if you got two new wholesale accounts while testing a new ad, that's notable!
6. Look at the intangibles—did you enjoy yourself? Did you connect with new people you like? Was it miserable?
7. Decide how (or if) you want to continue to use the tool.

SPECIFIC TOOLS

So far, we've talked about the general principles of sharing what you do online, because I want you to be ready to use any tool that might not even exist yet. All the same, let's talk about some specific tools.

Keep in mind that the first step to using any of these tools is to determine if your people use them, decide on the message you want to share, and then experiment with implementing it. Nothing I say about any of these tools is a must-do; these are only some tips to consider.

FACEBOOK
People tend to go to Facebook to to hang out with people they already know. And when the people they know recommend something, they're likelier to buy. So your presence on Facebook can take a few different angles—a personal account, a business page, and "Like it" buttons on your site and shop.

You probably already have a personal account. When you're using it, don't forget to mention what you do and what you make—and share pictures of it! There's likely someone in your personal circles who wants to buy a gift and what you make is perfect for them. If you use your personal name in your business name (Jane Smith Designs), you might find that many customers and fans (people you don't know) friend you on Facebook. It helps to have a personal policy about how you want to use your personal Facebook account and to stick with it. This will save you the time of agonizing over whether you should friend someone or not. However you choose to use it, embrace it and don't be shy about explaining it if someone asks.

No matter how "public" you intend to make your personal Facebook account (or what changes to the privacy policy they implement), do your best to keep your page unembarrassing. If your brand is for sweet, romantic grandmas, you probably don't a want a party-girl picture to be the first thing a Facebook-searching customer sees.

You can also have a Facebook page for your business. This helps you communicate directly with people who want to hear about what you're doing in your business. (Too much business stuff on your personal account might annoy your friends.) At the very least you can share links to your blog posts or email newsletters. I've found that many of my customers go to Facebook first to ask me a question. (They're already there, and it's where many people do all of their communicating.) Having a Facebook page helps them ask me, without having to friend me. (Remember: your customers might be just as reluctant to have you, a marketer, as a "friend" as you are to have them.)

You also want to make it easy for people to recommend your thing on their Facebook pages, so make sure you've got a Facebook "like" or "share" button on your items, your blog posts, and your site.

Using Facebook for your business is a mix of you reaching out to people and enabling your fans and customers to share what they bought. No matter what, make sure you don't use Facebook to send messages or "events" to everyone you know (either on your personal page or your business page). The Events feature should only be used for actual events, in a physical space that you're inviting people to attend. A website launch is not an event and sending it out as one will turn off more people than it attracts. The same goes for wall posts. Don't post on someone else's wall unless you're talking directly to them. Remember: people can mark you and your messages as spam and that will affect the way your other fans see your messages.

TWITTER

Unlike on Facebook, people on Twitter are already talking to strangers and to people they'd *like* to be friends with.

You'll get the most out of Twitter when you interact: reply to people and share what they say.

Just like Facebook, you can use Twitter to reach out and to give your users handles to share your products. Twitter is especially good for listening. You can ask questions (and get many answers in a short time) and use those answers to make your readers part of your business. Using a tool like TweetDeck or Hootsuite, you can create a stream around a specific search or a limited list of people. (When I find that one of my yarn buyers has a Twitter account, I add her to a special "customers" stream, which I check in with more often than my general stream.)

You can also use Twitter (which allows for more regular and random messages) to show who you are behind the business. It's not a problem to get "off-topic" from your business's focus (in fact, it's recommended) but make sure that what you're saying creates resonance with your business's message elsewhere.

FORUMS

There are a zillion different forums on the internet, all with different cultures and unspoken (and spoken!) rules. More than anything, forums are a tool for talking about a specific subject with people who are interested in that subject. Most are connection tools, not marketing tools (and if a bunch of people are sharing their message in the forum, it's probably not an easy place to stand out). Instead of trying to tell everyone on the forum about your thing, make an effort to get to know people. The people you meet might become your friends or your cheerleaders. In order to foster these relationships, listen to them, and talk about what the forum is about.

YOUTUBE

The video sharing site YouTube is the second largest search engine on the internet. If your thing can be demonstrated or explained, make a video and share it on YouTube.

Make sure your title is clear and descriptive. Use your product's name and the general name (like: *How to Use Handspun Yarn by Blonde Chicken Boutique*, or *How to Wear your EverFluffy Scarf*) and tag it with every word that has to do with the video. Put your link in the description (and in your profile!) and make sure you reply to every comment (but delete the mean comments and don't take it personally—it's just the YouTube culture). Better yet, make a whole mini-series of videos showing how to use your product (or if you're a fine artist, share short videos of your painting process). Keep the video under two minutes.

EMAIL LIST

Emails are a great way to keep in touch with your people. Setting up an account with an email newsletter system like Mail Chimp (my favorite), makes it easy to collect names, send messages to everyone and see what links the readers are clicking. Making your newsletter great and readable and clickable is an art form unto itself, but the best way to learn is to start noticing which emails you read and click on, and then practice with your list and your people.

A QUICK WORD ON TOOLS YOU MIGHT FORGET ABOUT

Email signatures: What do you want every person to know about your business? Include that in your email footer (set it in "signatures" in your email client). It should, at the very least, have a link to your site, and maybe one social media account.

Ads on other sites: Many popular sites have spots for advertisers in their sidebar. Before you go buying ads, make sure that your Right People read the site and will click on the ad. The site can provide some of this information, but dig up your own information too—ask your customers what their top five sites are and if they've ever bought anything from an ad.

Note: Don't buy an ad until you've got everything else in this book in place. You want to optimize everything else about your site, shop, and customer experience before you start buying traffic.

Blog: Everyone wants to know: Do I have to have a blog? The quick answer is: no. Unless you feel compelled to write weekly, don't feel compelled to start a blog. If you are excited about having a blog, then by all means, do it! Think about your ideal reader (if you want your blog to be a marketing tool, then this should be the same as your Right People) and provide information they want to read, not just info you want to share. What do they want to hear about your product? About your process? Blogs are a chance to invite your fans "behind the curtain." Do it in an interesting, entertaining, or educational way… and then stick with it. Building a blog audience takes as much work as building a customer base. Check out the Content Strategy section in Chapter 7 to figure out what to blog about.

Teaching online: Before considering this, ask yourself what your Right Person wants to learn. If you make bridal jewelry, perhaps you can teach a class for brides on matching jewelry to their dress and hair style, or about posing for their pictures. If you make scarves, perhaps you can teach about winter safety, or how to buy a scarf for someone else. To teach online, you'll want students, a platform to deliver the content (a free conference line, or an email list, or something more complex), and a registration system (ideally on a page on your website; check out e-junkie.com for creating a "buy" button that will automatically send the students the information). Diane of Craftypod.com teaches a class about teaching online, and that's a great place to start.

Google Places: If you run a bricks-and-mortar store (or sell at a physical location), make sure all your information is correct on Google Places. While you're at it, check out Yelp and FourSquare. You want to make it easy for everyone to find you—and for them to tell their friends that they're at your shop.

Whew, this has been a big chapter! You can use this chapter to do *whatever* you want to do online, to use *any* tool to share your message with your Right People. If you first think about your people, your message, your strategy, and *then* the tool, you'll be able to use any tool effectively. If you learn how to listen, connect and share on one tool, you can apply it to any other tool, online or off.

Is this shop approching the shop
for you?

3.Shops

Shopowner
Confidential

are you
ready?

2. craft
Show

Is this
one for
you?

make
the most!

OUT!
into the
world

1. Everyday

get comfortable
Saying it!

— taking
your
Message
out

— what to say?

where's
your LOCAL
RP?

CHAPTER 6: OFFLINE TOOLS, AKA THE REAL WORLD

Now that you've learned the basics of marketing online (listen, connect, and share), you're ready to market anywhere. In this chapter, we're going to look at getting your business out into the "real world." Just like in Chapter 5, we're going to look at the foundations of offline marketing so you can apply them to any situation. We'll end with some specific advice for getting your product on shelves and in your Right People's hot little hands.

Even if you're an entirely online business, don't skip this chapter! If you sell *physical* products, they're going to show up in the *physical* world, flying off your computer screen and into the shops, homes, and hands of your Right People. Even if (like me) you don't like to ever leave your studio, this chapter will help you decide where to spend your (limited) out-of-pjs time.

One last note before we get started: I'm a hermit, an introvert, a stay-in-my-pjs-all-day kind of artist and writer. I get nervous and fluttery **every** time I meet someone new. I'm awkward, nervous, and yet… getting out of my studio and going offline (doing craft shows, teaching, and just attending events with my Right People), has done more for my business than anything I did online. I've met customers (who have become long-time buyers), retail shops (who order and reorder), friends (who became evangelists) and even the publisher of this book (whom I got to know over some delicious ice cream at an industry event).

Now have I convinced you to go offline?

Through all of this, keep in mind that the same foundations apply whether you're talking to someone online or offline. You'll first want to think about where your Right People are and where they'll want to buy your thing. In this chapter, your Right People also include the people that can help you grow your business, like magazine editors, retail shop buyers, and people with influence over your buyers. So, you might attend events that don't have your buyers, but do have editors, publishers, and taste-makers (like an industry show, or conference, or a small-biz learning event).

No matter what kind of people you're looking for, as always, we'll start with your Right People and where they are. Before you spend time looking for craft shows or shops to sell your work, take some time to think about where your Right People are in your town. And don't worry! Once you know this, you can scale it to other towns and even other countries.

WORKSHEET: WHERE'S YOUR (LOCAL) RIGHT PERSON?

What are some of the shops in your town where she might shop? *(If you can only think of chains, do a quick Google map search of tiny, independent boutiques, galleries, and bookshops in your town.)*

What events might she attend? *(Is she likely to go to a craft show? A concert? A gallery opening? A baseball game?)*

What else does she do with her time? *(Go to church? Participate in the PTA? Play a sport?)*

If you've made some sales online, consider sending a quick email to your Most Right People and ask them where they shop in their town. Where else do they buy the kind of thing you sell? *(I'm amazed at my own buying habits—I buy more housewares in my local, organic grocery store than I do anywhere else.)*

Use these answers to find similar shops near you and while you're at it, contact the specific shops they list and say, "Your customer [Sue] thought my items would be a good fit for your shop. When's a good time to talk to you about it?"

YOUR MESSAGE, OFFLINE

After you have compiled a list of the places where your Right People would like to be buying your product, it's time to think about your message again. Just like we applied your message and brand to every aspect of your online marketing, we're going to do the same with your offline marketing. We're going to start by thinking about this generally and then get into the specifics of individual situations.

Now, how can you convey your message *in person*? Where in your communication style will that message show up (in part or whole)?

There are the visual cues:
- your appearance (fun? serious? expensive?)
- your business card
- your product packaging and label
- the printed material you bring: a wholesale catalog, flyer, or order form
- your display

The verbal cues:
- the language you use
- how you describe your product and your brand

And the non-verbal cues:
- body language
- friendliness
- confidence

I know, that's a lot of stuff! But don't get overwhelmed; instead, use this as a checklist for every live event or meeting you plan. Have a few lines about your brand (and each product) worked out, think through what questions the buyer might ask you (and have the answers handy!) and do whatever you have to do to feel fresh, friendly, and confident in what you have.

Just like with online marketing, you'll want to use every opportunity (whether it's an event, an in-person sale, or just a conversation) to listen, connect, and make your item shareable. For most of us, this comes naturally, as long as you treat it like any other conversation. The trouble comes when you start thinking *"Sell! Sell! This person is touching my stuff! Ohmygoodness!!! SELL!!!"*

When you feel that creep up your back and into your jaw, take a deep breath and listen. Ask the person a question (it could be related to your product, or not). Ask about the event, what they're wearing, or their hobbies. Just give yourself a little space to listen to them and to connect to something they care about. If their reply leads you to talk about your product, great. If not, just keep breathing and listening.

An example: When most people enter my craft show booth, I ask, "Do you knit or crochet?" If the person says no, then I know they're unlikely to buy yarn, so I'm just friendly and relaxed. If they say yes, I say "Oh, for how long" and then lead into, "Well, all the yarn you see here is made by me, this section is handspun… etc., etc."

As a *customer*, my best in-person buying experiences have happened when the seller engaged me about anything else and didn't talk too much about their product. This is a big difference between online selling and in-person selling (and stay with me, because I know it's going to sound obvious): in person, the buyer can *see* everything they need to see. They do not need you to spell it out for them. Online, your descriptions have to be thorough, engaging, and entertaining. In person, your labels should have the vital info (materials, size, a cute story about your business), and you only need to answer the questions they ask. It sounds obvious, but if all your experience has been selling online, it easy to forget that your job has switched from *explainer* to *engager*. You don't need to describe what's there, you only need to engage the person and continue to (gently) pique their interest.

Now that you've listened and connected, the last step is to make sure that everyone (really, *everyone*) can share your product and your work with anyone they know that might be interested in it. This can be as simple as making sure your mom and grandma have a big stack of your business cards to hand out as they gush about you to their friends, to having coupons to hand out to anyone who comes into your booth (*Oh, you're not a knitter? Well, take this coupon and give it to any knitter you meet*), to including your link and message on anything you hand out at an event or class.

Another way to make your work shareable is to have a simple, easy-to-remember thing that you say when asked, "So, what do you do?" For a lot of artists, this is the dreaded question. Where to start? What to say?

Especially if you have a day job, one that isn't your art… what do you say? Do you mention the art?

This is entirely up to you.

The more people you tell, the more people who will *know*, the more people who can share it with their friends. You don't have to tell everyone *everything*, but having a sentence or two can be the difference between a conversation that ends in "oh, OK" and a confused look, or "Hey, my wife loves purses, I bet she'd love to see yours."

This is where the message that you put together on page 34 comes in handy. Take it and rewrite it for different situations, using the next worksheet.

WORKSHEET: SHARING WHAT YOU DO, IN PERSON

Who should you give a stock of business cards to (the people who you know will really hand them out)?

What will you say when a stranger at a coffeeshop asks you what you do?

What will you say when your coworker asks about your craft?

What will you say when your extended family asks about your hobby?

What will you say when the magazine editor or retail shop owner asks what you do?

WALKING OUT YOUR DOOR

Now that you have some ideas of how you can take your online marketing skills to the offline world, let's get more specific. Let's talk about all the places you can take your real-world goodness and make sure your thing shines at every opportunity.

You came up with a list of places your people might be in your town. Grab that worksheet now because we're going to go through each and every venue and get you prepared to venture forth. You might share your thing in shops, events, shows, classes and just in your daily life.

SHARING EVERYDAY

Sharing in your real life is probably the easiest place for you to start. If you haven't talked to anyone face to face about your work yet, practice on your friends, family members, and pets before you go to a shop or sell at your first craft show.

Relax: you aren't trying to **sell** everyone your work, you're looking to enlist evangelists, people who want to spread the word for you. You want to empower them (with a stack of your business cards, or a sample of your work to wear) to tell all the people they know about what you do.

As much as possible, **wear** your work. Whether you make jewelry, handbags, or scarves, keep them on you. When someone compliments you, recognize that this person, the complimenter, is likely one of your Right People. Here, in the flesh! Keep yourself calm. Try not to slobber all over yourself at the pure joy of being recognized for the genius you are, but thank the person genuinely. None of this, *"Oh, THIS, ick, I made it, it's not as good as it should be… see my mistake here?"* And then follow up your gratitude with, "Thank you, I made it. I actually sell them." Gauge the response and if they seem interested, pass over one of those business cards.

If you don't make something you can wear (art, cards, pillows), keep your ear open for those inevitable "So, what do you do?" questions, or "What did you do over the weekend?" and fill 'em in on your crafty endeavors. Even better: if you're now selling at a shop or a craft show, be sure to tell everyone about the show or shop. It can be much more comfortable to talk about an event or a shop you like, instead of about you or your work.

PRINTED MATERIALS

This is a great place to think about your printed materials. Just like your online presence, you want your in-person presence to reflect your brand and your message. The most traditional way of doing this is with a business card.

Take a moment to think about the lowly business card, that tiny 3x5" slip of paper. It has so much meaning for a new business owner, doesn't it? It's often the first truly business-y thing you invest in. But notice how I didn't bring it up until now? I want you to wait until you've identified your Right People, your message and your web presence before you buy your cards because all of *that*—all the work you've done—will make a better business card.

While the card is a loaded, meaningful symbol for you—a symbol of the legitimacy and bigness of your business—it's just another tool. And it's one of the most overused tools in business (not to burst your bubble, but every secretary and dentist has a business card), so yours has to be *effective.* The most important aspect of it is that it does what you want it to do. To make sure it does that, fill out the following worksheet.

WORKSHEET: YOUR BUSINESS CARD

What do you want your business card to do? (Check one or write in your own goal.)

☐ Refer people to my shop where they'll buy something.

☐ Get them to call me, so we can talk. *(If you have an online business, this probably isn't it!)*

☐ Help people remember me and my product so they buy it when they need it.

☐ Get people to email me so we can talk.

☐ Help people find me on social media so we can keep talking.

☐ _____

What information will your card need to have on it for the recipient to do what you selected above? (Check one or write in your own goal.)

☐ website URL

☐ email

☐ phone number

☐ business name

☐ personal name

☐ Twitter/Facebook information

☐ tagline

☐ picture of your work (big or small?)

☐ picture of you

(Hint: it's VERY unlikely that you want all of these—remember, the more you have on there, the more confused the business-card-recipient will be about what you want them to do next.)

What aspects of my brand do I want to carry onto my business card:

Color: _____

Font: _____

Style of photo: _____

After you order your business cards, you can go crazy with other promotional material that can coordinate: postcards, posters, your product labels. For each piece, make sure that you're clear on WHO it's for and WHAT you want them to do.

WORKSHEET: WHO YOU ALREADY KNOW

What groups are you involved in?

List five specific people you know who would like what you make (a barista that always wears great jewelry, the pastor's wife).

1.

2.

3.

4.

5.

Do they know about your work?

How could you tell them in a way that doesn't feel icky?
(Role play for a minute. Imagine the entire conversation with each of the people.)

Don't worry: this isn't a network thing where I'm going to tell you to go talk to those five people and ask them for five more names. The only thing you need to do is pay attention the next time you're in conversation with those people. If they don't already know about your work, bring it up. You are not trying to sell them on it, you're just letting them know that you make stuff (and if you're right that your work is something they'd like, they'll be happy to hear about it and ask you more about it). If they show interest (and you've worked up the nerve) pull out one of your business cards and say something like, "If you wanna look at it, it's on my website."

Over the next week or so, notice all the people you come in contact with that are interested in what you're doing. You won't be selling all the time (that wouldn't be much fun), but once you start paying attention, you'll be amazed at all the people in your life—all the people who might want to help you spread the word.

Look around: You do *not* need to wait until you have your business cards in hand before you start telling people what you do. If you have some way for them to buy your thing (you take cash, or you have a shopping cart on your site, or an Etsy shop), you can start telling people. And trust me, you can bring it up a few times before someone will remember what you do and where they can buy it. *Who do you already come in contact with that might like what you sell?*

EVENTS

Now that you're a bit more comfortable talking about your work (*you have been talking about your work, right?*) you're ready to move on to talking to complete strangers. If your plan revolves around selling wholesale, then the next place you'll want to go is a shop. But if you're like most crafters I know, you'll want to sell directly to the customer for a while, before you grow into selling to shops. Events, craft shows, and farmer's markets are all great places to get started.

Actually, before we get into selling at events, let's talk about just *attending* the event. By "event," I mean anything where a large group of people are going to gather: a conference, a festival, a gallery opening, a craft show, or an industry event. There are a few reasons to attend these events before you start selling at them.

For starters, you can research and take notes. If possible, attend any craft show as a buyer before you become a seller. Notice what kind of sellers there are (if it's *all* jewelry artists and you sell jewelry… you may want to rethink it), and if it's all hand-made or a combination of mass-produced and hand-made (I skip these shows). Look, *really look*, at the booths you're drawn to. How is their booth set up? Where's their table? What does their banner look like? What first drew your attention?

Just as important, notice the booths that feel unwelcoming. What about them doesn't draw you in? What's the seller doing? How are the lighting and the displays?

Another reason to attend an event is, of course, to meet people. At a craft show, you might meet a fellow crafter who becomes a friend or partner. At a conference, you might meet a teacher, mentor, or a community of fellow crafters. At a trade event, you might meet editors, publishers, and shops that want to buy your goods.

Before you attend any event, make a few notes on what you want to do, whom you hope to meet, and what you hope to learn. To really prepare, head to Twitter and find other attendees and start to get to know them before the event starts. While you're at it, make some appointments or lunch dates so you make sure to hook up with everyone you hoped to meet.

CRAFT SHOWS

Every part of a craft show is marketing. From the show you pick, to your application, to how you actually DO the show, every part of it reflects your business, your brand, and your goals. In the next section we're going to go deep into knowing you're ready for a craft show, how to pick a craft show, how to apply to a show and how to do the craft show in a way that serves your marketing goals.

When you're first entering the craftybiz world, you'll notice that craft shows are everywhere. Every biggified craftybiz seems to be doing them and if you like people and you love talking, they might seem like the perfect venue. But before you send in your application, you want to decide if you're ready for a craft show right now.

(If you decide you're not, you can always come back to this section in a few months!)

DO YOU HAVE A STRONG FOUNDATION?

One of the most lucrative stages of a craft show is the week after it's all over. People who met you at the show check out your site and buy what they didn't have the money to buy at the show. If you don't have a site, a shop, and some products in stock, you'll miss out on these sales. We'll talk a bit more about having a strong home base below.

Can you afford the time and money?
Craft shows take a lot of time away from your usual business schedule. You create more products than you've probably ever had in stock at a time, which isn't just time-consuming but also expensive because you buy all those supplies without selling the items yet!

To decide whether you can afford this, do some math. Figure up the costs of the show you want to do (application fee, table fee, travel costs, anything extra you'll have to buy for a display). Now double it. Can you afford that right now? If not, that's OK, just start saving. You can save both money and product—go on and stock up your just-for-a-show inventory!

Can your thing be transported?
This question might seem silly, but it's important! Do you have the means of getting a large quantity of your thing to the site of the show? Will your customers be able to lug the thing home? In other words, will your thing—or two or three of your things—fit in the back seat of a tiny car? Or next to someone on the subway?

If the answer to both of these question is *yes*, it's time to start building your foundation.

BUILDING A STRONG FOUNDATION

Everything you've read so far in this book has helped you start building a strong foundation. Before you even apply to a show you'll want to have:

- a clear statement of what you do, a way to talk about it, and an awareness of why it's special (see Chapter 2 for a review)
- systems in place for taking money, tracking inventory, and creating on a schedule
- a place to send non-buying but interested people (a website, or a local shop that sells your work)

- a way to reach the buyers after the show (a newsletter sign-up sheet)
- something for them to do at your site (buy something? read something? connect with you?)

HOW TO FIND A CRAFT SHOW

When you know you're ready to do a show, you'll have to *find* a show. There are *many* kind of shows. The bigger shows are great but tend to stick with established crafters. One way to get into one of the bigger shows is to become an established presence at the smaller shows. Even if you *could* get into a big show, you want to start with something smaller so you can practice and learn. Try out different displays, products, and inventory on the smaller shows and get used to talking to your customers.

The best place to start with craft shows is to look at the ones that people you respect are doing. Check out someone who doesn't make exactly what you make (*or else the show organizers might not choose you, in order to maintain variety*), and look on their Events page (or sidebar) for the shows they've done or are going to. There are several craft show listing sites, but they change all the time, so try googling "craft show" and then click around.

Once you find a show that's near you and looks interesting, look up everything you can find about it: use Google blog search, Twitter search, and Flickr to see what people are saying about it, how many people are excited to attend, and to get an idea of what kind of prodcuts are sold there.

As you're searching, fill out the following worksheet.

WORKSHEET: IS THIS CRAFT SHOW FOR ME?

1. How do you feel about this show? What's your first impression?

2. What marketing is the show doing?

3. The show website—is it clear? Is it geared more towards vendors or shoppers? (*You* might want the vendor information, but it's more important for *shoppers* to find the information they need to attend.)

4. Cost of a booth—can you fit in enough of your products to earn back the cost of the booth times five? (Your goal will be to make more, but this is a preliminary starting point.)

5. Distance—is it reasonable for you to schlep your products that far?

6. If your thing is location-based (you sell classes or state-themed mugs), will your product make sense in this location?

7. Cost of travel—add it ALL up, right here (transportation, hotel, food):

8. The right market for your work—are your Right People here?

9. Are the name, logo, and marketing materials for this craft show in line with your Right People?

Have you found a show that you love and are excited to do?
Yay! Now it's time to apply!

APPLYING FOR A CRAFT SHOW

When you apply for a craft show your goal is to show yourself and your business in the best light and to make sure the organizers know why you're a good fit for their show. The number one way to do this: *fill out the application exactly as they say.* I can't stress this enough—no matter what they say in the application, just be sure to do it in exactly the order and the way they say. After you're completely clear on the instructions, the second step is to present yourself and your products clearly. This includes great pictures and clear descriptions. (Some shows will call this description your Artist's Statement.)

Your pictures should be clear, in focus, well-lit, and have nothing else in the frame. Make sure your images are big enough to be seen clearly, but not so big that they don't work as email attachments (this might take some experimenting). As you choose pictures to include with the application, pick ones that show the variety of what you make and sell. If you carry a range of prices, make sure to include both your lowest-priced item and your highest-priced item. (Both should look gorgeous and clear and well-lit!) When picking, focus on the pieces that best represent what makes you and your work unique. Remember all those worksheets from Chapter 2? This is the time to review them, and then choose the pictures of pieces that best represent that.

The last part of your application will be a description of your business (or the artist's statement mentioned above). If you don't do a lot of writing in your daily work, take your time on this. Write out everything you want to say first, then put it aside, and come back and edit it later. Send it to a friend for proofreading.

As you're writing, be sure to include everything you learned about yourself and your product in Chapter 2. Be clear about what makes you unique, what makes your product special, and what your customers really love. If it starts to feel long or wonky, go back through and pick three qualities you want to highlight (e.g., sustainable, colorful, easy-to-use) and just focus on describing them. Here, again, make sure that you're filling out the application exactly as asked. If the application says to write three sentences, only write three sentences (and don't make them ridiculous run-on sentences).

YOU GOT IN!

Yay! If you're here, it means you got accepted in a craft show! **FABULOUS!** You've got a lot to plan and prepare for, but instead of covering every last aspect of doing a craft show, we're just going to focus on using it for your marketing purposes. Outside of the scope of this book is your inventory management (i.e., how to make sure you bring enough, how to keep your online shop going during a craft show, etc.), pricing, and accepting payment.

Everything else about your show—and what we'll focus on here—is marketing. From the way your booth looks to the way you talk to people, from the label on your product to what you do after the sale. We're going to break it into three sections: Visuals, People, and Post-Show.

The visuals of your craft show

As you know by now, you want your brand to be reflected in everything you do. This includes the colors, the personality, and even the font. The biggest visual of your craft show is going to be your booth or tent: your banner, your displays, how much stock you have. The smallest visual are the tags on your products—do they include all the information your buyer will need? Do they reflect the personality of your brand? Everything in between, from the tablecloth on your table to the displays to the signs around the booth, should reflect your style and your personality.

Above all else, all of the visuals should highlight the unique qualities of your product. If you make hand-knit hats that look adorable when on a head, make sure you have lots of head-shaped displays. If you make dangly earrings, make sure your displays let them dangle. (For the love of gold, don't lay them down flat!)

People of the craft show

The people to focus on in your craft show are both the people *in* the booth (you and any helpers you have) and the people who *want* to come in the booth (the buyers and the curious). You want every person who walks into the booth to feel welcomed and delighted, so make sure that you and your helpers are friendly and well-versed in common questions. Take a minute before the show to think about the qualities of your brand and how you, your personality, and your attire can communicate those qualities. Then make sure you pass that information on to anyone else who works in your booth with you.

I have a checklist I run down with anyone who offers to help. (I'd rather not have "help," then have one of my volunteers treat a customer rudely.)

- Acknowledge every person who walks in the booth (even if they seem nothing like your Right Person).
- Smile.
- Be polite, *no matter what.*
- Ask questions. (I have two or three stock questions that we can ask anyone who comes in the booth.)
- Answer questions. (Have a few notecards with the answers to FAQs.)

POST-SALE

Even though this is what you do *after* the show, you still need to think this through *before* the show. It's vital that you put a few systems in place, so you can get in touch with the buyers (and browsers) when the show is all over.

A craft show isn't just a venue to sell, it's a place to share your work—even with those who won't buy it. You meet people, people who want to buy your thing, people who want to tell someone else about it, and people with large networks to share your work with (bloggers, journalists, editors, publishers). You are going to do everything you can to make it easy for everyone who *wants* to share it, to *actually share* it (irresistibly shareable, remember?).

The first step in getting someone who met you at a craft show to talk about your work is for them to *remember* that they met you. It might sound obvious, but the truth is most shows are overwhelming—so much good stuff, so many interesting people.

Sure, you'll give everyone a business card, but you also want to be able to remind them of you and your work later.

If someone at the show has a particular interest (*Do you sell this in red?*) or wants to talk to you about something in particular (*I write for this magazine and would love to feature your earrings*), make a note of it and gather all their information (name, email, phone number, best time to reach them). They

> Create a field in your email software that lets you record where you met the person. Make it a drop-down list and plug in your show, so that you can just pick the same answer for everyone you met there. This will make it super-easy to send a message to **only** the people at the show. (And let you know when you come back and do the show next year!)

might also sign up for the newsletter, but don't trust yourself to remember who they are or what they wanted. (I've learned this the hard way!) These are the very first people you should contact after the show. (Well, wait 24 hours, you don't want to seem desperate.)

The easiest way to help everyone else remember your work is via email. Sign up for that email management software (you did this back in Chapter 4, right?) and at the show just put out a piece of paper (on a clipboard, with a pen), with a column for names and a column for email addresses. (I like to "seed" the list with my name and email and that of a friend, so it doesn't look empty and unloved.)

Give everyone who signs up for it a discount (I like 10%, because it makes the math easy) on what they buy. When someone talks to you or seems interested but doesn't pick up something to buy, point them towards your sign-up sheet and say, "If you think you'd like to be reminded about that piece later, sign up for my email list."

You'll go home with a big list of names and emails, which will take just a bit of time to add to your software (your email software makes this easy). Within a week of getting home after the show, send out a short, friendly email with a reminder of where you met and a link to where they can find your work. If you send out a weekly or monthly newsletter, let them know what to expect and make it clear that they can unsubscribe at any time. (This is why you use an email management app; it will automatically generate an unsubscribe link and form, and you won't have to keep up with it at all.)

You can turn even the most staunch non-buyer (*I don't have any cash on me right now*), into a buyer if you give them the opportunity to shop from home, in their pjs, after the show. Make sure you're ready for these sales by having a well-stocked online shop (even if you take it down for the weekend of the show, pop it back it up right after), and a clear way of asking them. I'm not usually a fan of discounting my work, but I have found that a discount to everyone I met at the show (both at the show, when they sign for the list, and again when I email them) is worth it and makes the show that much more valuable.

Now that you've talked about your work to a zillion people at the coffeeshop and at some craft shows, you're probably feeling pretty comfortable. It's time to take that comfort into a shop and get your work on the shelves.

SELLING IN SHOPS

Even though we started with your everyday life, and then worked through craft shows before we hit the shops, it's entirely possible that you'll start with shops and you'll sell only wholesale. Even if you do want to focus exclusively on wholesale, it's always a good idea to get your work in front of people and learn how you want to talk about it before you hit up your favorite shops. In other words, if you skipped to this page first, go back and read the section on sharing your thing in your everyday life.

A quickie lesson on the terms shops are going to use, before we get into how to approach them:
- **Retail:** selling directly to the customer (this is what you're doing in your Etsy shop or at craft shows).
- **Wholesale:** selling to a shop that sells directly to the end consumer. Typically the wholesale price is 50% of the retail price. Usually, you (the seller) set a minimum order for shops to meet before they get the wholesale price. They place an order and then you invoice them. They have X days to pay after receiving an order (30, 60, or 90).
- **Consignment:** a shop puts your work on the shelf, and pays you only for what sells. You usually make slightly more than your wholesale price (60-70% of retail is common).

Now, if the thought of selling your work for 50% off what you currently sell it for freaks you out, then you want to rethink pricing. If it helps, think of it like this: the shop has to make a profit, too. They are saving you a *lot* of marketing and time by talking to *their* customers about *your* work.

ARE YOU READY?
Just like with craft shows, you need a strong foundation before you sell wholesale. Do you have an inviting home? Your home includes a website (with information on how the shop can buy wholesale), clear photos, and enticing descriptions. It also includes promotional materials that you'll use when you approach shops (a wholesale catalog, business cards, etc.) and that the shop will use to sell your goods (labels with all the information, a display for your products, etc.). And above all, you have to have a pricing structure that works for you and the shop.

Can you produce at high volume?
Remember that your shops are going to be purchasing a minimum amount of goods from you. For most handmade businesses, a $200 minimum is a LOT of items. Can you produce that many products in a timely manner? *While still sleeping and eating?* Before you go into the shop, have a plan

for how you'll fulfill their order and an estimated time when you'll have it done. This will put the shopowner at ease that they can trust you to deliver the order when they need it.

Can you afford it?

Have you set up your pricing structure to make a profit when you sell wholesale? To make sure you can afford it, start by setting your wholesale price, right from the start. It should include all your costs (including your time) *and* have an extra margin for profit. And then, when you determine that number, double it for a retail price. If you need to bring in extra help to fulfill the order, that cost needs to be built into your price as well. Selling wholesale has other associated costs (like the time to go to the shops, to maintain those relationships), but many crafters find it less expensive then selling retail, because they do fewer shipments (with more product in each shipment) and include less packaging in every shipment.

Do you have shelf-ready packaging?

Do your labels say everything you need to communicate about your product and your brand? Do they highlight what's special about you and what you do? Can your product sit on a shelf as is? Does it need to be in a bag or box or sealed? Does it have a short shelf life?

Are you comfortable talking about it?

If you've followed the path in this book, then you are very comfortable by now. If you jumped right from selling online (or just setting up your home) to approaching shops, you might be a bit shy still. Do yourself (and the shopowner) a huge favor and get comfortable before you ever walk into their shop. This might mean going back over Chapter 2 and practicing in front of your dog, or just striking up conversations with strangers and practicing your pitch. (This might scare off some people… but better them than a shop owner!)

PICKING A SHOP

Yay! You're ready! Now you just need to find a shop to sell to. You might already have some in mind, but before you approach them as a seller, go into the shop as a shopper. Notice what they sell, how they display it, and the price points. And then be a ninja and take a few notes either while you're there or right after using the following worksheet.

WORKSHEET: IS THIS A GOOD SHOP FOR YOU?

Do they carry other handmade items?

Do they carry local products? (*You can ask the sales staff this and note their reaction.*)

Do they carry your product category (earrings, yarn, notecards)?

If not, how will your product category fit in with what they already have, in the shopper's mind?

Where would they put *your* thing in their shop?

Do they carry anything EXACTLY like what you make?

What's the average price?

How close or far away is that from your average price?

List the three qualities that come to mind when you think of this shop:

1.

2.

3.

Are any of those in common with the qualities of your brand? If not, do you see your products fitting in here?

Did you find something you really LOVE here? Describe it:

Are the sales staff friendly? Will they represent your brand well?

If, after the worksheet, you're convinced that this is the shop for you, grab a business card and go. (And buy that thing that you loved and chat up the clerk… is it the owner? If not, how does she like working there?) When you're out of eyeshot, jump onto an internet connection and go to the shop's website.

- How is it?
- Do they list the brands they carry?
- Do they have their location information?
- A phone number?

If you like what you see (or you're willing to forgive a bad—or worse—non-existent website), give them a call! Before we dive into what to do on that call, let's cover some ways of checking out non-local shops.

FINDING A FAR AWAY SHOP

Call up or email your non-local friends and family (especially ones with a great sense of style) and ask them for their favorite shops. Visit shopping, fashion, or design blogs and look at the shops they highlight. But before you go calling the shop, you want to do the research. Look at their website. Do a Google blog search for anyone who's blogged about their experience, a Twitter search for the shop to see what customers are saying, and a Flickr search for pictures of the shop. Once you've got an idea of what the shop is like (and their customer service) try to find at least one person who has shopped there. Ask them straight up if your products would fit in the shop. Ask them to help you fill out the previous worksheet so that you're sure your products are a good fit.

TALKING TO THE SHOP

Now that you've found the shop, it's time to talk to them! This is the first impression the owner (or manager, or buyer) is going to have of you, so keep that in mind. A quick review of the website will tell you if the shop owner prefers to be contacted via email or phone number. (A clear hint: do they have their phone number or email address on every page?) If you call, make it early in the morning (right when they open) to avoid interrupting during the busiest time of the day. Before you get on the phone or send an email, fill in the following worksheet.

WORKSHEET: TALKING TO A SHOP

Shop name:

Phone or email:

Contact name:
(*If you've been able to dig this up ahead of time, you'll save a lot of trouble*)

A few times you'd like to meet that work for you (pick slow times; earlier than noon on weekdays is the safest):

1. Ask to speak with the person who finds new products for the shop.

2. Ask: *Is this a good time to chat for a second?*

3. Explain who you are and what you sell.

4. Tell her what you like about their shop or why you think your thing fits in.

5. Finish wish: *I'd like to come in and share it with you, does (date/time) work for you?*

Note: there are only five sentences here. Say those five sentences, and then wait for a reply! Do not go on and on about you, your work, OR the shop.
Confidence, friend! Confidence!

OK! Good job! The buyer is excited to meet you and you now have a time to come in and talk.

Remember to dress professionally and in line with your brand and the brand of the shop. Even if you're going into a tattoo parlor to sell your line of spiked chokers, dress in a way that shows you respect their time. Before you go in, be prepared to talk about the following worksheet.

WORKSHEET: FIRST MEETING WITH A SHOP

Now that a shop has agreed to meet with you about selling your thing, you will need to be prepared to discuss with them how you'll fill their order.

Don't try to sell the shop the MOST stuff possible; sell them what you think THEY will sell. It's far more advantageous to have a shop reorder from you regularly than have them make one big order and never sell out of your work. With that in mind, think about these questions:

When will you deliver their order?

How will you deliver it (mail or hand-delivery)?

What are all the options (colors, sizes, the best product variety that you think will suit their shop) that you can offer for sale at the shop?

SHOP OWNER CONFIDENTIAL: SEVEN THINGS BOUTIQUES WISH INDIE MAKERS KNEW ABOUT SELLING TO US
by Abby Kerr

As a former indie boutique owner, I had the privilege of developing many mutually beneficial business relationships with makers and designers both local to my store and from faraway. It was always a privilege doing business with those artists who understood their own value and respected my vision as a shop owner, and were able to hold both in equal measure throughout our relationship.

For makers who want to sell to brick-and-mortar stores, learning the ins and outs of selling is a matter of experience, experimentation, and natural savvy. Going straight to the source (shop owners!) to ask questions and considering every bump in the road a teachable moment are two ways to get ahead of the game.

Here are seven things we shop owners wish you, as a designer, knew when it comes to selling to us:

1. If we love your work *and it's right for our store*, we'll go to great lengths to get an appointment with you. Great shop owners, like editors or art buyers or corporate headhunters, set their sights on who they consider to be the 'next big thing' (or the next amazing indie talent) and don't lose focus. If you come across our radar and we are highly interested, getting in touch with you becomes a high priority. Prequel to this tip: implement Tara's marketing strategies for coming across our radar.

2. We are busy, wear many hats, and are highly distractable during store hours. Also, we may be stressed out, worried, tired, under the weather, annoyed by our last customer, and our feet may be sore. Please understand this and try not to take personally any 'edge' or 'blasé-ness' we may present. For this reason, *drop-by appointments are usually not a great idea*. Take Tara's advice and research our store, then contact first by email or phone to see if we'd like to schedule an appointment with you, or if we simply would like linesheets emailed to us.

3. *A 'no' should never be taken as an indictment of the quality of your work, your personality, or your presentation style.* A 'no' means your work simply isn't the best fit for our store's mix at this time. There's only so much floor space and so many selling seasons in the year. Smart, savvy, experienced shop owners curate a merchandise mix that is likely to sell through expediently and they attract their Right People through the door over and over again. There is always room for the 'next' and the 'new' in this mix, but it may not be your line. Your line may be incredibly awesome, but may not work in the mysterious and idiosyncratic algorithm that makes our store tick.

4. You don't need to oversell your work to us. The quality and/or functionality of your work should sell itself. An old-timey, 'hard sell' style has no place in modern-day retail. Shop owners are regular people just like you. We want to be talked to with respect, courtesy, humor, and in language we understand. Anything that feels too puffed up or overzealous can ring false. Keep it real and rational and let your Right People Retailers gel with you in a natural way.

5. We appreciate dealing with vendors who *follow through, keep their word, and don't overpromise but slightly overdeliver.* Even though you may develop a friendly rapport with a retailer, remember that *this is business.* A casual sales and relationship tone is great just so long as the surefire follow-through is there to match. If you promise a catalog, send one. If you say you'll call to see how your line is doing for us, pick up the phone. No need to promise the world, but be sure to come through with just a smidge more than we bargained for and you'll come out ahead of most vendors we deal with.

6. We don't expect you to cater to our every whim or customize your work to fit our store concept. (Unless we are inexperienced or have an air of entitlement, in which case you probably don't want to do business with us anyway.) You, like any good retailer, have a vision for your business, too. *Don't compromise your values in order to land an account.* Don't bend over backward and exploit your work in order to make it fit with someone else's vision. Your Right People Retailers already love your work just the way you love to make it.

7. We appreciate being kept in the loop with your line, whether it's a postcard in the mail announcing your tradeshow schedule, a free sample of a new product, or an email with your next season's linesheet attached. If we are already customers or have intimated that we're thinking about buying from you in the future, keep sending materials until we ask you to take us off your contact list. You never know when we'll be 'open to buy' in your category and that new item you introduced is exactly what we're looking for.

YAY! YOU GOT THE ORDER! CONGRATULATIONS!

As you fill the order, deliver it, and *support your retailers*, remember to keep up everything you've learned so far:

Right People: As you meet your Right People in other settings, be sure to tell them where else they can find your work. If the shop is local, give them directions and tell them to tell the shop you sent them.

Website: Be sure to include all your retail shops on an easy-to-find page on your site. Even better, include a picture of your display in the shop and a link to directions. (Google Maps makes this easy.)

Online marketing: Tell all of your social networks that your work is now in this new shop—but wait until you have confirmation that your order arrived! Include a link to the shop or directions.

Listen: Ask your retailers regularly (a month after they place an order) what you can do help them. Perhaps they need ideas for displaying your goods, or they'd like a little sign to hang up that tells more about your unique production style.

Connect: Offer to connect with the shop's customer base. A trunk show, a class on how to style your bridesmaids, or even a book club. Be the person who brings customers to the shop; don't leave it all up to them.

Make it shareable: Do your tags have all the information the buyer needs to understand your brand? What else can you add that will make them want to share it with their friends? (Hint: a great story is easy to retell.)

In this chapter you've walked through sharing your work with a few people and grown into selling in person and in shops. If you read through this chapter all in one sitting, it might seem a little overwhelming, so take a minute and choose just one thing you want to do NEXT. This might be the first chapter where you didn't fill out all the worksheets at once… and that's OK. Remember: you can always come back and do the next step.

In the next chapter, we're going to put it all together. You're going to look at your larger strategy and then fit in all the pieces you've learned so far into one big, glorious plan for your future!

STRATEGY + PLANS

put it all together!

Big Vision

Targets!
- goals
- What do I want this to do?

Marketing Objectives

Marketing Strategy

Place
Product
4Ps
Price
— Promotion → Content Strategy

Action!

daily   weekly   monthly

CHAPTER 7: STRATEGY

Now it's time to pull it all together: your message, your people, the tools you want to use. We are going to make it all-purposeful (and put it onto your calendar) with a marketing strategy. In a traditional (i.e., big business) marketing strategy, you start with corporate objectives—those goals that the entire business is working towards. In your (i.e., tiny business) marketing strategy, it's a good idea to start in the same place. Begin by looking at your big vision for your business (and your life) and then at how that can turn into specific marketing objectives. Those marketing objectives get turned into marketing *strategies*—the kinds of things you'll do (and experiment with) to reach your objectives. Like most businesses with an online component, your business' marketing strategy will include a content strategy. We'll wrap all this up by using the tools you've already learned about to reach your goals and get it all into a do-able, daily (weekly and monthly) plan.

BIG VISION

We're going to zoom *way* out and look at the big picture. How do your business, your message, your people, and YOU fit together? The big questions (and bigger than what this book can cover) are: *what do you want from your life? And how does your business fit into that?*

The good news is, *you don't have to know everything* (ah, the annoying part is: you *can't* know everything! Oy!) but it helps to have a bigger picture of what you want to happen in your life and how your business can support that.

This next bit is very you-specific, so most of the first section is examples and worksheets. I promise that we'll get back to learnin' and doin' after you figure out the Big Picture.

WORKSHEET: INTENTION + VISION

Your marketing plan should help you achieve your long-term wishes and hopes.
So who are you?

What's your life filled with?

What would you *like* it to be filled with?

How will your business provide you with that?

In a magical world, what would your business do for you?

Some more things to consider as you think about the big picture and your business:
How do you like to interact with people? In large groups? One on one? From the safety of your studio, with your pjs on?

What do you like your daily life to be like?

Doing many things in one day? Doing one kind of task/day (administrative Wednesdays, studio Tuesdays, etc.)

Do you want to work every day? Or just during certain hours?

Keep in mind that you do not need to **choose** from these examples. Your expectations, dreams, and goals will be different from everyone else's and instead of trying to fit into some mold, please take the time to define this for yourself.

A few examples:

Arlene is a graphic designer but wants to be spending her time making her art—not designing for clients. She and her cats live simply, but she wants her art business to support her in a comfortable lifestyle. She's got all day to work on her business and because she loves painting and drawing, she wants to spend lots of time on her art.

Lela is a new mama. She wants to be able to support her entire family from her business so that her husband can go back to school and pursue his passions. She wants to live debt-free, own her home outright, and have lots of cushion so that she could (one day!) take time off of work and travel. Because she has a tiny baby, she can't spend endless hours creating. She needs to be able to make her products in a short time-bursts and handle all the administrative tasks in even shorter bursts. Her business needs to fit into the two hours a day she has while her baby naps.

Tamara has a day job and hates it. She wants her business to make enough to replace her salary. She and her husband have joint finances, but her salary makes up three-quarters of it so she can't just quit and let his job pay for everything. Right now she can only work on creating products in the evenings and the weekends, but she she can do administrative stuff during her lunch break at work. She dreams of a day when she can work on her business full-time, but for now, that's a fantasy. Her strategy has to fit into her available time, and it has to grow her business to the place where it can support her family.

Jude is a retired grandpa. He wants to spend his days playing with his grandchildren and his evenings working on his craft. He loves meeting new people at craft shows, so he wants to expand until he can get into his favorite shows, but he doesn't need the business to pay all of his bills. He doesn't want the business to feel like work, since he's worked for enough years... but he is willing to learn new things, meet new people, and fill his evenings with growing his business, up to a point.

So, one of the questions you need to ask yourself is: what is YOUR big picture?

WORKSHEET: BIG PICTURE, SPECIFIED

What does success look like, for you, in your dreams?

If all of your marketing were perfect and everyone was reached and everything sold… what would that look like? What would it *feel* like? What are the Ideal Fruits of all this labor?

What metrics would you measure? (numbers, money, sales?)

Why those?

How much money would you be making (per year / per month / per week)?

What does that metric look like…
In a year?

In six months?

In a month?

In a week?

What is happening in your Ideal Business…
Next year?

Each month?

Each week?

Each day?

TIME

Yeah, I know, there's never enough time! But, in an ideal world, how much time would you spend on the different tasks in your business?

When you're thinking through what you want to spend time on, remember all the small stuff *and* the fun stuff. Include any of the following:

- making
- writing
- connecting
- reading
- researching
- labeling
- shipping
- in-person selling
- strategizing

WORKSHEET: TIME SLICES

List everything a typical week would include:

Now slice up the pie with how you spend your time.

How do you currently spend your time in your business?

How do you WANT to spend your time?

ENERGY

It's easy to see how your business will take up your time, but don't forget that it also takes energy. Creativity takes energy—mental energy, physical energy, even spiritual energy. And you, my dear, are human and do not have an unlimited supply of energy.

Creativity is cyclical. In work/life/business, there are these crazy full-of-ideas periods, followed by amazing get-stuff-done periods, followed by… not-creative stuckness, tiredness, I-don't-wanna-ness.

The cycle affects individual ideas and general, day-to-day creativity. For me, it starts with an idea, then a flow of ideas, then I get in the flow of making the ideas happen. This revving-up is my favorite part of the cycle. I would live here if I could, but then I get anxious to DO, to implement.

The apex of the cycle is not just the flow of ideas, but the production, the work, the actual doing. In other words, the creating. But after that apex, as the projects continue to roll forward and the rush of ideas turns into a rush of details, sometime in the midst of *doing*, I slow.

And soon, the slowing is the overwhelming characteristic. No longer creating the thing, I'm either introducing the thing to the world or I'm slowing down in the middle of the thing.

Following the slowing, comes the fallow period, the not-doing time. For a lot of us, this fallow period is not fun and we try to skip it. We try to go right from the slowing, back to the doing.

But this doesn't work. The ideas aren't there. You can't jump right back in the flow.

Before I recognized that this is a stage in the cycle, I kept pushing.
- pushing to get ideas
- pushing to work on projects
- pushing to work work work
- pushing to get out of the un-doing and back to the doing

But pushing like that gets to you.

When you stop, refill, and respect the cycle… the cycle cycles back. Inexplicably, inexorably, unequivocally the ideas come back. First, just a trickle, then a stream, and then a rush and you are back. Back to doing, to planning, to *creating*.

Whether you push or not, your creativity will cycle. When you recognize the fallow period, when you respect it, when you rest in it, then you create a blank space, a well that is soon filled again with ideas and energy.

Recognizing the flow of your own cycle is an important piece in figuring out your strategy. If you know that you cycle between high energy and low energy every week—or every month—you can plan accordingly. If you ignore your cycle, you'll schedule things at times that just **don't** work for you.

WORKSHEET: IDENTIFY YOUR CYCLE

Looking back on your last project, how long did the full-of-ideas period last?

How long was it before the bored-with-doing-this part start?
If you can't remember, or you're thinking, "What? That never happens to me!" then just take note of your next project (maybe even working through this book?). About how much time passes between full-of-ideas and really-tired?

Now that you know this, how can you work WITH this?

What would your schedule look like if you respected this?

GOALS

The second part of your Big Picture are your goals. These are closely tied to what you want from your business and what you want your life to look like. But the difference between the Big Picture and your goals is that goals are can be split up into measurable milestones. Your goals are those things that you'll be able to point to and say *"Hey, I accomplished that!"* From getting your first sale, to getting into that big craft show, to being featured in a magazine—these are goals.

We're talking about goals here because it's the next step in figuring out your bigger strategy. While you may have a general overview (*Quit my day job! Be happy! Spend my time crafting!*), if you don't know *specifically* what you want, you won't be able to create a strategy to get you that.

Remember the goals are not the destination!

Even after you reach a goal, you won't be done!

You'll have new goals and different directions.

But this is good news! It means that you can pick to work on ANY of your goals, knowing that you'll get to your other goals in the future. It means that you can change your milestones and your goals (and even your dreams) any time you want.

And it also means that maybe, when you reach your goal, it won't be as fabulous as you had imagined, because in the *getting* there you learned a lot and changed and now want something new.

And that's OK. It's part of the journey.

WORKSHEET: BIG GOALS AND DREAMS

Remember: we're talking BIG, long-term, crazy-far-away dreams, so go wild!

Where do you want to sell your products?

How much money do you want to make in an awesome month of your business?

To have the kind of life you identified in the Big Picture worksheet, what would have to happen (sales, money, oppurtunities)?

What press would you like to receive?

At the apex of your success, what will your product line look like?

Which of these goals can you reach in...

In a year?

In six months?

In a month?

In a week?

For each of the above, try to pick something specific and measurable. "A lot" isn't measurable. Twenty-five is measurable.

MARKETING OBJECTIVES

Now that you know where you want to take your business, the next step is to create some marketing objectives that will help you reach your big dreams for your business. Marketing objectives focus specifically on your marketing (which, as we talked about in Chapter 1, is communication with your customers that moves them down the path from hearing about you to buying from you), and what you want your marketing to do.

Traditionally, marketing objectives are expressed in terms of a metric you want to change (sales, market share, repeat customers) and the number (or percentage of change) you want to reach. Traditional marketing focuses on things like "brand awareness" (which they measure through extensive surveys) and "market share" (how much of the market is buying their brand versus another customer). Even if these kind of metrics are out of the reach of your tiny crafty businesses, the idea of marketing objectives is still useful.

Marketing objectives help you focus your marketing (and keep you from being sucked into an endless loop of tweeting and emailing) and give you measurable goals to work towards. Instead of "market share," your small business is probably more concerned with easy-to-measure metrics like "number of new customers," "number of repeat customers" or "size of average order."

To create your own marketing objective, think back to your big dreams and goals. What kind of sales would you need to reach them? How much would you have to grow? How many more customers would you need to have?

The best marketing objectives relate to something measurable about your sales or actions that your people take, because it keeps you focused on the numbers that reflect the health of your business.

Warning: it's easy to get sidetracked by measuring things like page hits or Twitter followers or blog comments, but these not are effective marketing objectives.

Why?

Because they don't tell you anything about your profits, losses, or conversion rates.

Instead, look at those page stats and compare them to how many sales you have.

- How many hits to your site = one sale?
- What's the correlation between your number of comments and your number of sales?
- Does a popular page lead to more sales?

Measuring this kind of connection will also educate you on which parts of your website could be more effective. If a particular item in your shop gets a lot of page views, but doesn't sell, experiment with it! Rewrite the description; change the pictures; change the price.

Remember: it's possible to have a very *popular* business that doesn't make any money!

WORKSHEET: WHAT ARE YOUR MARKETING OBJECTIVES?

Pull out your Big Goals and Dreams Worksheet from page 137. In order to reach your big goals, what one or two things do you need to change?

Pick one or write your own:
- ☐ sales per day
- ☐ sales per month
- ☐ average total of an individual order
- ☐ conversion rate from consumer to customer (divide your number of unique page views or subscribers by the number of buyers in a given period of time)
- ☐ percentage of customers that become repeat customers
- ☐ number of items in an individual order
- ☐ number of new customers in a month
- ☐ number of repeat customers in a month
- ☐ average number of times that shops reorder
- ☐ number of months before a shop reorders
- ☐ profit on each item sold
- ☐ number of stores my product is sold in

Before we can talk about improving the above metrics, you need to know where you are now. From the items you circled above, what is their current status? (For example, *I have two sales per month,* or *I only make one sale for every 200 page views on my site,* or *the average total on an order is $30.*)

How would you like the above metrics to change? Better yet, pick a specific *number* that will represent change. (For example, *I want to double the number of orders per month,* or *increase the average number of items in an individual order to five,* or *sell 1,000 bars of soap every month,* or *increase repeat customers to 20% of total sales.*)

Quick reality check: Would the change you identified above truly represent an increase in your profit? For example: if you wrote in that you want to be in three new shows this year, but you haven't yet earned a profit at craft shows, that goal isn't going to do much for you. Instead, find an improvement that matters (say, your profit of the average show).

MARKETING STRATEGIES

If you filled out the previous worksheet, you're probably thinking a bit differently about your marketing now. Instead of just trying to get "more people," you can see what that means for your sales, your profit, and the health (and sustainability) of your business. You may have even noticed that some of those metrics had nothing to do with just *telling* more people about your thing and are instead about adjusting some other aspect of doing business.

And that brings us to turning these marketing objectives into marketing *strategies*. Strategies are what you do to bring a *product* that your people want to *those* people.

Traditional marketers break these strategies into the Four Ps:

- **Product**
- **Price**
- **Place**
- **Promotion**

As we've discovered throughout the book, marketing isn't just about spreading the word or getting more people to buy, it's also the product you sell (and its packaging), the price you sell it at (and the value you communicate through that price), the distribution method you use (the place—online, in shops, at craft shows, etc.), and every way you communicate your message to your people.

Let's start at the top and work our way through the Ps to see how they can turn into strategies that will help you reach your objectives.

PRODUCT

Most crafters start the process (and this book, and their business) with their product firmly in mind. Dryden makes jewelry. Amy makes art. Kristine makes knitting patterns. But when we talk about "product" in marketing, we mean everything that has to do with your product: the individual item, the collection of products you make, the packaging, the label—all of the branding.

While you might already know what you make, there's a big swath of possible products within that category. Dryden can make plastic earrings, dangly earrings, bridal jewelry, spike chokers or gold wedding bands. Amy can paint murals or miniatures, squid or monsters or flowers. Kristine can design lace shawls or striped hats or traditional gansey sweaters. Each of these choices is a marketing decision because each choice will reflect what a different market (or group of Right People) will want. Each choice will create a different brand, will necessitate different packaging, and will lead to a different result.

Before you start looking at what you'll change about your product, look at where you are now. What do you offer? Who are you offering it to? What's your marketing objective? What could you alter to reach that objective?

When you're looking at products in your marketing strategy you'll want to think about what you already know about your Right People (or the people you want to be reaching) and what your marketing objective is. Where the two meet will inform the creation of a new product, a new line, or getting rid of a product.

PRICE

Way back on page 29, we established that price is not a *benefit*. You don't want to sell at the lowest price; it's just not sustainable for a small business. However, price is part of your marketing in that it communicates something about value to your people. Selling fashionable jewelry, hand-forged from precious metals, requires a higher price in order to be trusted and taken seriously. If you see a gold, hand-made ring for $10, you immediately doubt its genuineness. The price communicates the value of your time, the value of your materials, and the value of your skill and sensibility.

You can also use price in your marketing strategy to create a new line of products or reach a new market. Perhaps your line of $200 handbags could include a smaller, less expensive line of change purses and wallets. This helps you reach new customers who then might opt to buy an expensive handbag once they experience the quality of your work, and it might increase the size of the average order. (If your shopper is already spending $200 for a bag, what's another $25 for a matching wallet?)

It's easy to focus on *growth*—what new thing we want to create, how we can get in more shops. But sometimes the best way to reach an objective (and grow your business overall) is to *stop* doing something or *start* something small. You can delete a product from your collection, create a new line of lower-priced items, or take your products out of a store that's not serving your needs.

I stopped stocking my Etsy shop because I realized that it didn't have the best return on time invested. (All that photography and listing!) Instead, I offer one yarn per month to people who have signed up to hear about it and I sell in larger quantities to yarn shops.

That means I'm only making the products that someone has already purchased, I spend less time on taking photos… and I don't even have to blog (my customers hear from me via email and my retail customers don't tend to read blogs).

As you think about creating strategies around price, take a look at what you have so far. Do you have a range of prices? What's the average price? Does that reflect a healthy profit?

And now think of your Right Person: what else might she want in the form of price? Is there a new market that you'd like to reach? How can price get you there? Be careful that you don't just assume that less expensive is better. For many brands, the addition of a more sophisticated, expensive product line introduces them into a new, more profitable market.

PLACE

The *place* where your people can buy your products is a vital (and pretty unglamorous) part of marketing. Think about it like this: if your Right Person can't find your thing, how can she buy it? For many crafters, the place they sell their work is online, either in an Etsy shop or through their own website. This choice (between an Etsy shop or your own site) is a marketing decision. Both options say something about your brand, and about the market you're trying to reach. Of course, you can always start on Etsy and eventually move to your own website. Even the set-up of your shop is a marketing decision; how do you split up the collections? What do you call them? How much clicking does a buyer have to do before they've purchased your item? How many pictures (and how big?) do they see? Most of all: is it easy to buy something from you? Is the process clear and obvious?

Place also refers to all the physical places your product is found. From the shops that carry it, to the craft shows you vend at, each of these decisions is a reflection of your brand and carries a marketing message to a particular kind of person. (This is why we did so much research in Chapter 6, before we approached a craft show or shop.)

Above all, the place your item is found directly determines what group of people come in contact with your work. If your jewelry (or shawls or art) appeals to a group that's not online, then you want to focus your **place** strategy on offline venues. If your Right Person never strolls through boutiques and does all her shopping online, than you want to have a clear, easy-to-buy-from online shop.

Where does your Right Person shop? What marketing objective can be reached by changing your place?

We're talking about *promotion*, which is communicating that you've got something that people want. **But who are you communicating TO?**

In traditional marketing, the broadcasters (people with a message, people who wanted to promote something) bought access to the buyers via commercials on radio and TV, ads in magazines and newspapers, and trailers at the beginning of movies.

This kind of promotion both interrupted the experience and was one-sided (just coming from the promoter). The internet (and social media) gives us a way of communicating with our buyers without interrupting them (instead, we've got their permission to have the conversation) and without being one-sided (they can talk back in comments or via social media). Best yet, we don't have to buy that attention; it's given willingly.

How do we get it?

You get attention by creating products and content that are both interesting and shareable. You give people something to share (a blog post, an email newsletter, a tweet, a video) so they have a reason for giving you their attention. And what you do with that attention is guide them down the path from stranger to buyer, all with the power of your content.

Your content strategy helps you build an audience (a group of people who want to read what you're sharing) and your audience is who you'll be communicating with when you have a promotional message to share.

PROMOTION

Now, this is what generally comes to mind when people think about marketing: promotion! Communicating the benefits of what you make to your people. Descriptions, coupons, sales… it all counts as promotion.

The **promotion** part of your marketing strategy takes everything that you've learned so far about how your message dovetails with what your people want to know from you *and* how you communicate that everywhere—from your website, to your email list, to social media to in-person events.

Up until now, we've talked about it in the general sense, but it's time to get specific. It's time to figure out what you're saying, when you're saying it, and where you're saying it. This is your **content strategy**.

CONTENT STRATEGY

Content is the *what* of what you're saying. It's what's on your website and blog, in your emails, tweets, updates, and product description. Your *content strategy* is your plan for how you're going to say all that. Your content strategy is what gives you a plan and schedule for what you say online. It includes what and when to blog, what and when to email, what and when to tweet, even what you have on your home page.

Even though we didn't call it a content strategy when we covered it in Chapter 4, some of your content is strategic. It is a one-time, set-it-and-forget-it thing (like your About page, or your home page). What we're going to dig into now is your recurring content, the stuff you need to create on a regular basis.

What

In order to be effective, your content needs to both convey your message and be interesting to your Right People. While you might find the process of making your item fascinating, your Right Person probably doesn't. Your Right Person might love to cook and garden and read information about that, but unless you sell something related to cooking and gardening, you likely don't want to build content around that. The overlap, the sweet spot of content, is where *what you want to communicate* about your product and brand lines up with *what your Right Person wants to read about it.*

Many crafters have trouble coming up with this kind of content and default to writing about what they like to read about… and instead of attracting Right People end up attracting a lot of fellow crafters. So how do you break out of this?

You pull out your worksheets, of course! Check your worksheets from Chapter 3 and use them to fill in the following worksheet.

WORKSHEET: CONTENT STRATEGY—THE WHAT

What does your Right Person read (off- and online)?

What topics do those sources cover?

What does a buyer need to know about your product?

What would she be most interested to know? (*What's unique about what you sell or how you make it?*)

What do you want to communicate about your product?

What do you want to share with your people?

What do your people want to read about?

As part of your bigger content strategy, from time to time, you might want to create content about things that appeal to your Right Person even if these topics are not directly related to your goals. You just want to make sure that you balance what she wants to read and what you want to say.

Let's look at examples at how your and your Right People's interest can overlap.
Amy makes art based on favorite sci-fi/horror characters like Cthulhu and Dracula. Her Right Person likely reads fan-fiction magazines, shops at the comic book shops, and is a bit geeky about other science fiction and fantasy stuff. Amy wants to communicate the quality of the materials, the goofiness of the subject matter, and how buying a bit of this art for the geek in your life will make their day. Her content strategy could cover topics about the newest fan fiction, her favorite Cthulhu stories (and how they inspired her new line of cards), or reviews of the top five Dracula movies (along with examples of how each Dracula influenced her artwork).

Kristine sells knitting patterns to knitters. Her designs look fancy (lace shawls) but are actually simple. She has a knack for making complicated things easy-to-understand and that's reflected in her patterns. Her Right People are knitters who want to start making lace shawls, but might be a bit nervous. They want to read about tips for their level of knitting (just past beginner), and they love to see other people's projects. She needs to communicate how easy her shawls really are, while demonstrating her skill at simplifying complicated stitches. Her topics could include tips (videos, pictures, tutorials) on how to do some of the intermediate stitches, highlights of what other people have made with her patterns, and a series on how to know if a project is right for you.

Specificity, please
Now that you've got a list of possible topics, there's still more digging to do. Topics are general—too general for your plan. In order to be interesting and to keep creating content week after week, your content needs to be specific. Each piece of content isn't just an *overview* of the topic, it's a viewpoint—your viewpoint—on one angle, or one aspect of the bigger topic.

Your angle includes *who* your writing for, your *experience* with the topic, and what you want to say about it.

For example, we can talk about the general topic of fashion, but it'll be much more interesting (and I can write endlessly about it) if I write about fashion *specifically* for new moms, from the perspective of someone who only buys handmade, and believes that a piece of clothing shouldn't cost more than $100.

WORKSHEET: WHAT TO WRITE ABOUT, SPECIFICALLY

Let's take one topic from your list and turn it into smaller, more specific content ideas.

The topic:

What five sub-sections of this topic could you write about? (*e.g., if my topic is sustainable yarn, my sub-sections could be different fibers—cotton, wool, etc.—specific environmentally damaging practices used for some fiber, and the specific research I've done.*)

1.
2.
3.
4.
5.

List three perspectives you could take on one of these sub-sections. (*e.g., I could highlight* **controversy**—*take one side of an argument about the topic;* **conciliation**—*try to reach agreement between two opinions about the topic; and* **my experience**—*what I've experienced and felt about the topic.*)

1.
2.
3.

Don't be afraid to be opinionated. What do you believe about the subject matter?

How can you share this information (*e.g.., interviews, stories, lists, links to resources*)?

1.
2.
3.

And now, to get even more specific, list five headlines for pieces of content you could write for that single sub-section:

Take these questions and apply them to all your topics!

Where

Now that we know the what, let's talk about the where. This is different for every business, but the first step is to think about your Right Person (as always!)—Where is she going to be looking for you? Where can you tell her more about you, your company, and your products? Where do you want to have conversations with her?

A short list of possibilities:

- **a blog**—regularly updated information that appeals to your reader
- **emails**—using the email software you set up in Chapter 4, you can send messages weekly, monthly or some other time frame
- **guest posts on other blogs**—write for someone with a bigger audience; just make sure their audience includes some of your Right People
- **social media**—Twitter, Facebook, Google+, Pinterest, forums, and many, many others
- **sidebar**—yep, even the stuff in the sidebar of your website is content
- **traditional publishing**—articles in magazines, stories in your local newspaper, even a book!

Where you choose to create content will be based on what your Right Person reads and what you're comfortable writing.

When

Once again, you're going to look at both what your Right People want and expect and what you're comfortable creating. Whether you choose to blog weekly or daily, tweet hourly or minute-ly, or email weekly or monthly, just make sure to be regular about it. Your audience wants to know what to expect and to trust you to meet their expectations.

Look at where you are now—how often do you create content for your people? How are they responding to it? And then look at your marketing objectives—If you get a new order every time you email, but you only email once every 2 months, how will you want to change? And when you *do* switch to more regular emails, do you still get the same rate of purchases? How do your conversion rates change as you change your content?

WORKSHEET: CONTENT STRATEGY—WHERE + WHEN

Where do you currently create content?

How do your readers respond to it?

Where else might your people want to read your content?

Where will you create content to reach your marketing objective?

How often will you post new content in each place?

Reality check: How much time per week will the above plan take you?
Remember that creating content isn't just about writing; it's also all the technical details of formatting and posting.

WORKSHEET: MARKETING STRATEGY WITH 4 Ps

This is the heart of it. This is where you begin to take everything you've learned so far and turn it into something for your business. This takes a lot of thinking, so set aside some time to fill this out. Give yourself the time and space to think it out and then come back to it over the next few days.

Rewrite your marketing objectives here (so you've got them front and center!):

Product:
What do you offer now?

What could you change about your product offering to reach one of your marketing objectives?

Price:
How is your current pricing strategy reflecting your brand and people?

What could you do to create a strategy with price?

Can you reach a new market? Offer your current market something else they want?

Place:
What segment of your Right People is your current place reaching?

Which of your marketing objectives can be reached by changing your place?

What will you change about your place?

Promotion:
Visit the Content Strategy worksheets on page 144 and page 148. Share your conclusions:

What topics will your content cover?

Where will it show up?

TURNING IT INTO A PLAN

Now it's time to take all of your strategies and turn it into action. You've listed ideas and strategies and goals but now you need to know when it will all get *done*. How will you move from where you are to where you want to be?

Depending on your planning style (I'm a staunch non-planning planner myself), your plan will take on different forms. You can create lists (for daily activities and weekly to-dos) or you can put it all on your calendar (or you can do both).

No matter your style, we all start in the same place: with the big picture and goals, broken down into some sort of timeline or plan. Some of your goals are do-able in a month, while some will take six months to a year. Some of your strategies involve daily to-dos, while others are more big picture planning.

Start with the big, long-term things and pull out a calendar. When do you want to reach each goal? How long do you have before now and then? What are all the smaller things that need to happen between now and then? Where can you fit them in on the calendar?

Next, look at specific dates and times that are outside of your control (like the deadline to apply to the craft show, or the date you'll do the craft show) and plug those into the calendar. Then list everything you need to do to get ready for those events. Where do they fit in? Whether you like to put everything on a calendar or in a list, just make sure you've accounted for everything you'll need to do to prepare for a hard deadline.

Once you've got the long-term planning (and have broken it up into short-term tasks), look at your regular tasks. What do you have to do to keep up your business each month? How often do you need to create your products, photograph them, write descriptions for them? How often will you ship? Where does that fit in your week?

And then it's time to look at your regular, reoccurring marketing messages. Your content strategy should inform how often your going to create it. Just make sure you have a way of remembering this and find a place for it in your schedule.

WHY A CALENDAR IS A GREAT MARKETING TOOL
by Diane Gilleland

So you have a small business. You have stuff to market, and you're marketing it with online tools or offline tools (or both). And at the same time, you have products to make, and new items to design, and emails to return, and shipping to do, and trips to the bank. How easy is it for your marketing tasks to slip to the bottom of your To-Do list?

Very.

And don't feel bad about that, either—marketing can feel a little intimidating even on the best of days. The trick is to break it down into nice little tasks, and then even more importantly, get them scheduled on a calendar. If you plan your marketing tasks in advance, they feel more like part of your workday and less like "that scary thing I really should be doing."

Not only that, but with a little advance planning, it's much easier to maintain a consistent and interesting marketing message, whether you're using online tools or offline ones.

GETTING STARTED
Get yourself a one-month calendar, for next month or a future month beyond that. Whatever type of calendar you use most is fine – a paper wall calendar, daytimer, or online calendar. Now, on this calendar, mark your important marketing events for the month. A marketing event might be an actual event, like a class you're teaching, a sale in your online store, or a new product launch. Or, it might be an "event" you create in order to build a little excitement around your product, like a coupon promotion or your cut-off date for holiday orders. Every business is different, but generally speaking, I think two or three marketing events per month is plenty—any more, and you run the risk of trying to say too many things at once and muddling your marketing message.

STEP ONE: SCHEDULE THE ANNOUNCEMENTS
As Tara has so beautifully said in this book, when you have things to market it's usually best to tell a story about them. Even so, there also comes a point in your marketing where you just need to give people the critical information in a rather no-frills way. Let's get these marketing tasks on our calendar first.

For the sake of example, let's say one of your upcoming marketing events is a big craft show where you'll be selling your handmade goods. You've marked the date of this show on your calendar. Now, how many days before the show would it make sense to remind people to come to the show and visit you? Three days, maybe? Four? On your calendar, then, schedule a day during the week leading up to this event where you'll make some simple announcements, like a blog post or a few tweets or a Facebook update inviting your people to the show. (Generally, one announcement post is sufficient on a blog. For Twitter or Facebook, however, you may want to schedule several announcements at different times of the day.)

STEP TWO: SCHEDULE THE STORIES

The next step in our calendar-making is to spin some stories that add color and interest to our marketing events. You've already been working on expressing how you and the things you make are awesome, so you also have some building blocks for these stories.

Stories help your people feel connected to you and your business—and we humans love a good story so much more than we love being advertised to, so it's important to schedule some storytelling that more subtly points to your upcoming marketing events. Look at each of your marketing events, and look for the related ideas that would make interesting stories.

Here are some examples of what I mean:
- Let's say your marketing event is a new product launch. Well, that lends itself to stories about how you came to design this product. It lends itself to stories about the people you've designed the product for. It lends itself to stories about small aspects of the product—why do you use that particular clasp? Why is this fabric better than that one?

- If your marketing event is a cut-off date for placing holiday orders, the stories might be about what goes on in your studio as you make products. How do you organize your materials? What are your working habits? What kind of music helps you work better?

- If your marketing event is a class you're teaching, the stories might be how you came to learn all about the subject you're teaching. They might be stories about how your readers can use the knowledge they'll gain in the class. Or you might tell some stories about your past students and how they experienced the class.

How do you communicate these stories? Through blog posts, Facebook posts, tweets, sharing photos on Flickr, through your email newsletter—whatever methods you enjoy using. On your marketing calendar, schedule 2-3 story-based posts in the ten days leading up to each of your marketing events.

OPTIONAL STEP THREE: DROP IN SOME TEASERS

Lastly, you may want to schedule a few small "teaser" posts in your calendar. These should happen 2–3 weeks before each of your marketing events. These teasers might take the form of a photo that reveals a tiny glimpse of a new product, or a post about how excited you are about your "secret project." A teaser might also be an "early bird" announcement, encouraging your people to sign up for a class or mark their calendars. Depending on the marketing event, teasers can help build some anticipation so that when you start telling stories and then announcing, you'll have the full attention of your people.

Not every marketing event needs teasers, of course—a cut-off date for orders, for example, wouldn't. But a new product launch, an upcoming class, or a big sale could all benefit from teasers.

WHEN YOU PUT IT ALL TOGETHER...

Look at your filled-in marketing calendar now! See how these overlapping teasers, stories, and announcements intertwine to form a varied and interesting stream of content? The story posts keep things from being overly marketing-based, and the teasers build interest, and ultimately, everything points to your marketing events. Best of all, you now have just a couple of small marketing tasks to do each day—and that feels *way* less intimidating.

Like everything else in your marketing, how you choose to plan and implement your strategies is a reflection of your strengths. I've included a lot of different tools (and the perspective of my planning hero, Diane) with instructions on using them. Pick a few to try out but they aren't *rules*—if they don't work for you, try something else. Experiment. If one set of tools doesn't help you remember to do what you want to do, or it just doesn't inspire you to action, try something else.

No matter your style, make sure you're thinking through three different aspects of planning:

1. **New projects**—These move you toward your big goals and include stuff like creating a new product line, reaching out to a new shop, or experimenting with a new content strategy.
2. **Keeping in touch**—This is your content strategy and your reaching out to customers. It includes all the content you regularly create to welcome in new people and the contact you make with new customers (thanking them for their order, asking for their feedback).
3. **Regular outreach**—This is getting out of your home (or website) and showing up in other places: Twitter, Facebook, a knitting group.

HOW I PLAN

I use a combination of a daily list (it includes the stuff I do for my business everyday), chunking time (two hours for writing every morning, shipping orders once a week), and revisiting my lists of projects I want to work on. Each week I list out the projects I'm working on that week and I list all the actions I need to take for each project (this includes writing promotional blog posts, emails, tweets.) Then I draw a (crude) little calendar for that week and fill it in with a general idea of when I'll do what. If I'm filling a particularly big wholesale order then sometimes whole days will be blocked off to spin and dye. Each morning, I glance over my little week and I write up a list of what I'll do that day, in a loose schedule format. It's not always the same as what I planned, because I like to go with my flow and some days I'm just not suited to do what I had planned to do.

When I first started marketing my yarn business, I wrote up a quick list of the marketing tasks I would do everyday. At the time, I didn't have any readers, followers, or buyers, so I focused on creating content for my site and then reaching out to new people. Now that I have more buyers and more commitments, I spend less time reaching out and more time responding to what's coming in.

Wherever you are in your business and no matter your goals, pull out your worksheets for this chapter and start to lay them out in a plan.

WORKSHEET: TURNING THE BIG PLANS INTO ACTION

Pick one task from your **Marketing Strategies worksheet** (on page 149):

- If it's a quick thing to change or do, write in a date when you'll do it (and put it on your calendar!):

- If it's a longer project, list out the possible tasks that will complete the project:

Does any part of your list rely on you doing a recurring activity, like writing a series of messages, or building a blog readership?

If so, how often will you do those things?
- ☐ Daily?
- ☐ Weekly?
- ☐ Monthly?
- ☐ Everyday for one week?

Put those recurring activities on the appropriate to-do lists, then do this for every one of your big goals!

DAILY MARKETING ACTIVITIES

Fill this in with the recurring activities that you'll do everyday (or nearly everyday). This can include any of the 4 Ps: *Product* (creating, listing), *Price*, *Place* (reaching out to new places), and *Promotion* (creating content, sharing a link to what you made).

You can view samples of other business's forms at TaraSwiger.com.

WEEKLY MARKETING PLAN

Fill this in with the activities you want to do weekly. Assign each activity a day of the week or just put it in the "sometime this week" section.

Even better, pull out your calendar and put it in for a specific appointment!

MONDAY

TUESDAY

WEDNESDAY

THURSDAY

FRIDAY

THE WEEKEND

ANYTIME THIS WEEK

MONTHLY MARKETING ACTIVITIES

What are the activities you only need to do about once a month?
List them here:

Visit this worksheet each week and schedule each of your activities on a specific day for this month!

DARLING, YOU'VE DONE IT!

You've defined your message, you've identified and started to find your people, and you've created a strategy for using both online and offline tools.

CONGRATULATIONS!

After doing a little happy dance and buying yourself a fancy drink—you deserve it—take a breath and… dive back in. Your marketing strategy and the system of moving new people into your business is a continuous process. Listen to your people. Tweak your message. And keep setting new goals and experimenting with strategies.

And tell me how it goes.

ACKNOWLEDGMENTS

On my 29th birthday, I decided I needed some big goal, a huge project to take me into my 30th year. What one thing did I want to accomplish before my 30th birthday? This book. I hoped and wished to sell the idea before June 3rd, I had no idea I could hold a finished book in my hands by then. That impulsive, unresearched dream only became a reality through the support, confidence, and patience generously given by every single person in my life. I can't begin to thank everyone I've ever had a conversation with (but be assured—you did shape this book!), but I gotta start somewhere.

Shannon, you took a meek "Is there a book in here?" email and turned it into something more fabulous, more genuinely me than I had ever hoped for. You literally made my (literary) dreams come true. Thank you.

Diane, your sharp eye and probing questions have made me a better writer, a better teacher and a better thinker. Thank you.

Amy, Kristine, Lori-Ann, and everyone in the Starship—thank you for being my guinea pigs and my first readers and my constant cheerleaders. You are the wind beneath my spaceship.

Thank you, Secret Treehouse for teaching me that compassion and me-ness don't have to be at odds with a smart business.

All my gratitude, dear family, for giving me just want I needed.

Mom, you make me believe that I can change my life at any moment, that I can choose a new path (and be happy) every day. Thank you for that and thank you for letting me read all day instead of going outside to play.

Grams, you taught me to say, "I could make that!" and I never stopped.

Thank you, Dad, for saying, "You haven't failed at self-employment until you quit and get a job. Everything other than that is a success." just at the moment I needed to hear it.

Cathi, you continue to teach me to embrace those Wetherby traits: independence, stubbornness, and thinking I'm always right—you make them seem downright lovable.

Justin, Troy and Dylan, you are hilarious and ridiculous and weird and I love you for that. You make me laugh when I want to be serious, and you remind me that at the end of the day, no matter what the Internet tells me, I'm still just Sis (to be ignored, harassed, and teased).

Jay, it's silly to even try to put into words all there is between us. I wouldn't have become the Blonde Chicken, and then the teacher, the writer or the Tara that I am without you. You have been, and always shall be, my friend.

APPENDICES
RESOURCES

CONTRIBUTORS

After founding Copylicious, Kelly Parkinson began to work with teams whose content had fallen down the chimney. Now she builds Content Dreamhouses and gives workshops so content feels as good for others to experience as it feels to create. Find her at Copylicious.com

Abby Kerr is a former nationally award-winning indie boutique owner, a fiction writer, and a coffee shop aficionado. She's a digital copywriter who teaches indie creative online entrepreneurs how to develop their voices in the marketplace. Find her at Abby Kerr Ink: abbykerrink.com

Diane Gilleland produces CraftyPod, a blog and podcast about making crafts and DIY media. She's published several ebooks to help crafters use online tools more effectively to market small businesses.

BUSINESSES WHO GENEROUSLY SHARED THEIR STORIES

Kristine Beeson is a giggly geeky crafty girl living in Vancouver, WA. She is a knitwear designer that delights in "designing a story in every stitch," with captivating techniques and an ultimately stylish piece. kadyellebee.com

Amy Crook uses her mad graphic artist skills to create handmade greeting cards, monster-themed coloring books, and original abstract art. Visit her online home at AntemortemArts.com.

OTHER PEOPLE I REFERENCED

Havi of FluentSelf.com
Chris Brogan of ChrisBrogan.com
Shannon of PolymathDesignLab.com
Dryden of DesignatedDryden.com

BOOKS TO READ

RUNNING A BUSINESS BOOKS

Handmade Marketplace, by Kari Chapin—if you don't yet have a business, start here for all the details on getting started selling your craft.

Boss of You, by Emira Mears and Lauren Bacon—my favorite business book for the past-beginner, not-yet-a-corporation sized businesses.

MARKETING-ISH BOOKS THAT FOCUS ON BIGGER BUSINESSES (BUT CONTAIN LOTS OF USEFULNESS!)

Trust Agents, by Chris Brogan—building a listening station and creating trust with your community.

Duct Tape Marketing, by John Jantsch—the essential marketing book, focused at slightly-bigger businesses

Ignore Everybody, by Hugh MacLeod—more about social objects, social capital and how to ignore everybody.

Booked Solid, by Michael Port—focused on consultants and service providers, this book taught me how to start with what you offer before you think of other people.

QUESTIONS TO ASK YOUR PEOPLE

- Have you used something like this before?
- What was your experience with this?
- Tell me about your favorite handmade item.
- What's your favorite color?
- What's your favorite flower?
- When do you start your holiday shopping?
- Do you buy Valentine's Day gifts?
- What was the last thing you bought yourself?
- How did you find my shop?
- Tell me about yourself.
- Have you ever bought any of my products in the past?
- How do you use them?
- What kind of information would you like about {fill in the blank with your product}?
- What do you like about {my product}?
- What 3 things could I do to make it better?
- What 3 things could I do to make it easier for you to buy?
- Tell me a story. What memories do you have about {product category}?
- When do you buy {this kind of product}?
- Do you ever search for {this product}? If not, how do you find it?

LIST OF QUALITIES

Adventurous
Agility
Anticipation
Beauty
Big Picture
Bold
Bright
Caring
Cheerful
Colorful
Comfort
Compassionate
Courageous
Creative
Curiosity
Dark
Dedication
Delight
Detail-Oriented
Discovery
Driven
Eco-Friendly
Effervescent
Enthusiasm
Elegant
Exciting
Expansive
Experimentation

Exploratory
Familiar
Fashionable
Fearless
Feminine
Festive
Flexible
Flow
Focus
Frivolous
Fun
Geeky
Girly
Grace
Graphic
Gratitude
Harmony
Ingenuity
Innovative
Joyful
Kind
Light
Loose
Loud
Loving
Lustrous
Luxurious
Masculine

Ordered
Playful
Powerful
Quiet
Quirky
Radiance
Restful
Rhythm
Sanctuary
Serious
Silly
Simplicity
Soft
Somber
Spacious
Sparkly
Structured
Support
Sustainable
Sweet
Tiny
Tranquility
Trusting
Twee
Warmth
Welcoming
Wonder

ABOUT TARA SWIGER

Tara Swiger is a writer, maker, and Starship Captain in Johnson City, TN. She explores creating smart businesses through her own yarn company, Blonde Chicken Boutique, and by serving as First Officer and Community Manager aboard creative, crafty and downright adorable ships (from tech start-ups to copywriters). She creates tools (the Map-Making Guide) and spaces (The Starship) for teeny tiny crafty businesses to explore their own best businesses and marketing plans.

Join the adventure at TaraSwiger.com

ABOUT COOPERATIVE PRESS
PARTNERS IN PUBLISHING

Cooperative Press (formerly anezka media) was founded in 2007 by Shannon Okey, a voracious reader as well as writer and editor, who had been doing freelance acquisitions work—introducing authors with projects she believed in to editors at various publishers.

Although working with traditional publishers can be very rewarding, there are some books that fly under their radar. They're too avant-garde, or the marketing department doesn't know how to sell them, or they don't think they'll sell 50,000 copies in a year.

5,000 or 50,000. Does the book matter to that 5,000? Then it should be published.

In 2009, Cooperative Press changed its named to reflect the relationships we have developed with authors working on books. We work together to put out the best quality books we can and share in the proceeds accordingly.

Thank you for supporting independent publishers and authors.

Join our mailing list for information on upcoming books!

COOPERATIVEPRESS.COM

CPSIA information can be obtained at www.ICGtesting.com
Printed in the USA
BVOW051606110512

290016BV00002B/1/P